C000212623

# ROYAL YACHTING ASSOCIATION

# AROUND THE RED TAPE

## AN RYA HANDBOOK OF LAW AND ADMINISTRATION FOR SAILING AND MOTORBOATING CLUBS AND SCHOOLS

by

EDMUND WHELAN

Barrister-at-Law

RYA
1987

ISBN 0 901501 31 X

Printed by Blackmore Press, Shaftesbury, Dorset

# CONTENTS

Page

INTRODUCTION                                              1

### I — THE CONSTITUTION
1.  Name and Objects                                      3
2.  Officers                                              4
3.  Trustees                                              4
4.  Membership                                            5
5.  Management Committee                                  6
6.  Powers of the Committee                               7
7.  Disciplining of Members                               8
8.  Byelaws                                               8
9.  Conduct of Meetings                                   9
    9.1   Quorum                                          9
    9.2   Chairman                                        9
    9.3   Validity of meeting                            10
    9.4   Minutes of previous meeting                    10
    9.5   Matters arising                                10
    9.6   Rights of audience                             10
    9.7   Resolutions, motions, amendments               11
    9.8   Proposal of motions                            11
    9.9   Seconding of motions                           11
    9.10  Amendments                                     11
    9.11  Questions                                       12
    9.12  Points of order                                 12
    9.13  Shortening a debate                             12
    9.14  Abandonment of debate                           12
    9.15  Adjournment                                     13
    9.16  Disorder                                        13
    9.17  Any other business                              13
    9.18  Voting                                          13
    9.19  Closing the meeting                             14

### II — INCORPORATION OF A CLUB
1.  Advantages and disadvantages                         15
2.  Name                                                 15
3.  Articles and Byelaws                                 16

| | | |
|---|---|---|
| 4. | Directors, Meetings and Accounts | 16 |
| 5. | Limited liability | 17 |
| 6. | The process of incorporation | 18 |

### III — LIABILITY IN CONTRACT AND TORT

| | | |
|---|---|---|
| 1. | Contractual liability | 19 |
| 2. | Tortious liability | 20 |
| 3. | Occupiers' liability | 21 |
| 4. | Litigation | 21 |

### IV — POTENTIAL LIABILITY TO THIRD PARTIES

| | | | |
|---|---|---|---|
| 1. | Club as organiser of races | | 25 |
| | 1.1 | Liability in negligence to competitors | 25 |
| | | 1.1.1 Laying the course | 26 |
| | | 1.1.2 Racing in foul weather | 26 |
| | | 1.1.3 Provision of safety equipment | 27 |
| | | 1.1.4 System of inspection | 29 |
| | | 1.1.5 Provision of escorts and/or patrol craft | 29 |
| | | 1.1.6 Seaworthiness of competing yachts | 29 |
| | | 1.1.7 Competence of competitors and their crew | 30 |
| | 1.2 | Defences to negligence | 31 |
| | | 1.2.1 Volenti non fit injuria | 31 |
| | | 1.2.2 Negligence not causing damage | 32 |
| | | 1.2.3 Contributory negligence | 32 |
| | 1.3 | Contractual liability | 32 |
| | 1.4 | Defence to contractual liability | 32 |
| | 1.5 | Liability to crew of competing craft | 33 |
| | 1.6 | Liability to third parties | 33 |
| | 1.7 | Joint negligence | 33 |
| 2. | Other sources of liability | | 34 |
| | 2.1 | Launching vessels | 34 |
| | 2.2 | Organising escorts, rescue etc. | 34 |
| | 2.3 | Team races | 35 |
| | 2.4 | Crew registers | 35 |
| 3. | Exclusion and exemption clauses | | 35 |
| | 3.1 | Children and Juniors | 38 |
| 4. | Limitation of liability | | 39 |
| | 4.1 | Launching | 39 |
| | 4.2 | Merchant Shipping Acts 1894/1979 | 40 |
| | 4.3 | Occupiers' liability | 40 |
| | 4.4 | Escort and rescue craft | 41 |
| | 4.5 | Duties in organising races | 41 |

## V — INSURANCE

1.   Buildings   42
2.   Contents   42
3.   Cash   43
4.   Loss of profits   43
5.   Employers' liability   43
6.   Fidelity guarantee   44
7.   Public liability   44
8.   Personal accident   44
9.   Piers, jetties and pontoons   45
10.  Club boats   45
    10.1  Limitation of liability   45
    10.2  Value of vessel   45
    10.3  Proposal form   45
    10.4  Periods of validity   46
    10.5  Standard policy   46
    10.6  Territorial limits   46
    10.7  Items covered   47
    10.8  Change of ownership   48
    10.9  Exceptions   48
    10.10 Chartering   48

## VI — LICENCES AND PUBLIC ACTS

1.   Licences for the sale and supply of alcohol   50
    1.1  Procedure for registration   52
    1.2  Objections to the grant of a certificate   53
    1.3  Permitted hours   54
    1.4  Inspection   54
    1.5  Licensing   54
    1.6  Special hours certificate   55
    1.7  Exemption Order   55
2.   Lotteries and raffles   55
    2.1  Small lotteries incidental to exempt
         entertainments   56
    2.2  Private lotteries   56
    2.3  Societies' lotteries   56
3.   Fruit machines   58
4.   Performing Rights Society   58
5.   Data Protection Act 1984   59
    5.1  Principles   60
    5.2  Enforcement   61
    5.3  Appeals   61
    5.4  Registration   61
    5.5  Exemptions   62

6.   Health and Safety at Work Act 1974                   63
7.   Fire Regulations                                      64
     7.1   A club licensed or registered to sell alcohol  64
     7.2   All clubs                                       64
8.   Offices, Shops and Railway Premises Act 1963          65
9.   Firearms regulations                                  67
     9.1   Starting guns                                   67
     9.2   Distress signals                                67
10.  VHF                                                   68
     10.1  Ashore                                          68
     10.2  Afloat                                          68

## VII — CLUB LEASES

1.   Distinction between lease and licence                 70
     1.1   Covenants                                       70
     1.2   Rent reviews                                    71
2.   Termination and renewal of tenancies                  72
     2.1   Landlord and Tenant Act 1954                    72
     2.2   Landlord's notice to terminate a tenancy        73
     2.3   Tenant's application for a new tenancy          74
     2.4   Grounds of opposition available to landlord     75
           2.4.1  Breach of repairing obligation           75
           2.4.2  Persistent delay in paying rent          75
           2.4.3  Breaches of other obligations            75
           2.4.4  Availability of alternative
                  accommodation                            76
           2.4.5  Possession required for letting          76
           2.4.6  Landlord's intention to demolish or
                  reconstruct                              76
           2.4.7  Landlord's intention to occupy holding   76
     2.5   Order for new tenancy                           77
     2.6   Compensation                                    77
3.   Dealings with landlords                               77
     3.1   Crown Estate Commissioners                      77
           3.1.1  The role of the District Valuer          78
           3.1.2  Conditions affecting the
                  Commissioners                            78
           3.1.3  Facility for public use                  79
           3.1.4  Restriction on mark-up                   79
     3.2   Water Authorities                               79
4.   The right to lay permanent moorings                   80
     4.1   Methods of dispossession                        81
     4.2   A land owner's right to claim rent              82

4.3   Who can stop you laying a mooring in tidal
      water?                                          82
      4.3.1   Department of Transport                 82
      4.3.2   Crown Estate Commissioners              82
      4.3.3   Planning Authorities                     82
      4.3.4   Harbour and marina owners               84

## VIII — CHARITABLE STATUS

1.   Income tax                                        85
2.   Corporation tax                                   86
3.   Capital gains tax                                 86
4.   Inheritance tax                                   86
5.   Rating reliefs                                    86
6.   Charity law and sport                             86

## IX — A SUMMARY OF STATUTE LAW AFFECTING CLUB-OWNED CRAFT

1.   Passengers                                        89
2.   Pleasure yachts used entirely for private purposes  89
3.   Pleasure yachts let on charter                    90
4.   Club launches                                     91
5.   Teaching establishments                           91
6.   British Waterways Board                           92
7.   Load Line Regulations                             92
8.   Boatman's Licences                                93
9.   Log books                                         94
10.  Powers of District Councils to license vessels    94
11.  Classification of ships                           94

## X - FINANCIAL ASSISTANCE

1.   Sports Council                                    97
     1.1   Amount of grant or loan                     98
     1.2   Conditions                                  99
     1.3   Sports participation grants                 101
2.   Local Authority                                   101
3.   Regional Tourist Board                            102
4.   European Community                                102
5.   Brewery                                           102
6.   Internal fund raising                             103
     6.1   Bonds                                       103
     6.2   Interest-free debentures issued by an
           incorporated club                           103
7.   Sponsorship or patronage                          104

## XI — CLUB MAGAZINES

1. Libel                                    105
   Defences to libel                        105
   1.1  Justification                       105
   1.2  Fair comment                        105
   1.3  Qualified privilege                 106
   1.4  Unintentional defamation            107
   1.5  Statutory defence                   107
2. Copyright                                108

## XII — TAXATION

1. Income Tax                               109
   1.1  Mutual trading                      110
   1.2  Fund raising and sponsorship        110
   1.3  Charities                           111
2. Value Added Tax                          111
   2.1  Taxable supplies                    112
   2.2  Input tax                           112
   2.3  VAT Accounts                        113
   2.4  Zero-rated supplies                 113
   2.5  Exempt supplies                     113
3. Rating of club premises                  113
   3.1  Person liable for rates             114
   3.2  Gross, net annual and rateable values  114
   3.3  Moorings and floating vessels       114
   3.4  Principles of valuation             116
   3.5  Appeals                             117
   3.6  Rate relief                         118

APPENDIX 1
Abandoned boats on club premises
(Page 119)

APPENDIX 2
Specimen set of rules for a yacht club
(Page 123)

APPENDIX 3
Agreement for the charter of a pleasure craft
(Page 145)

APPENDIX 4
Licensing Act 1964
(Page 150)

APPENDIX 5
Trust deed for the trustee ownership of club yachts
(Page 160)

APPENDIX 6
Media Guide
(Page 162)

APPENDIX 7
Health and Safety at Work Act 1974
(Page 171)

APPENDIX 8
Form of Loan Note issued by an incorporated club
(Page 172)

APPENDIX 9
Public Enquiries
(Page 176)

APPENDIX 10
Role and organisation of the Royal Yachting Association
(Page 188)

APPENDIX 11
Inspection of insurance certificates by clubs managing racing
(Page 192)

# INTRODUCTION

In publishing this, the first-ever handbook of law and administration for sailing and motorboating clubs and schools, the RYA hopes to cater for a long-felt need among the many hundreds of volunteers who take on the increasingly complex task of club administration. While the book is aimed primarily at yacht clubs, much of the information and advice applies equally to sailing schools, particularly those run partly on a voluntary basis. Indeed, throughout the book, there are lessons to be learnt by anyone having an interest in the administrative side of the sport.

The enormous increase in legislation in recent years and the ever-rising tide of liability claims which threaten anyone organising recreational activities, particularly those with an inherent element of risk, make it essential for the club administrator to have access to comprehensible advice on the relevant law and practice. To ignore the potential dangers is not only foolhardy but may also land the volunteer's fellow members in trouble if an injured litigant chooses to take action against the club as a whole as well as the individual club officers.

This book attempts to set out, in logical sequence, the solution to the many legal and semi-legal problems facing the secretary and treasurer of a club. Whether the club is incorporated as a limited company, or left unincorporated, the prudent administrator handling the club's day-to-day business or advising the committee on the practical implications of its decisions should always be aware of the legal pitfalls. When dealing with club premises, suppliers of food or drink, the provision of services and management of staff or convening meetings and organising races, statute and common law will inevitably impinge upon the administrator's freedom of action and he ignores these factors at his peril, and that of his colleagues.

Although the law is undergoing constant change, the RYA has decided to publish this book in a permanent rather than loose-leaf form because of the practical difficulties involved in keeping a loose-leaf publication properly updated. This first edition will inevitably omit many topics of interest to

1

club secretaries and the editor will be grateful for any suggested improvements or additions that can be incorporated in the next edition.

It is hoped that as well as being a source of information to those involved in the administration of sailing clubs and schools, this book will also be a source of comfort and reassurance.

Edmund Whelan                                    October 1987

# I

# THE CONSTITUTION

A club may be defined as a group of people acting together for a common social purpose. Although a club may be formed on a quite unstructured basis with no requirement for any legal formalities, as soon as property of any sort is acquired, or any contract for property, goods or services is contemplated, the law will imply common rights and liabilities between the members. As the activities of the club increase, and involve dealings with outsiders, so the rights and liabilities of the individual members become ever more relevant.

Any club which intends to own property or enter into dealings with third parties should adopt a formal constitution for the avoidance of doubt and the peace of mind of its members. This constitution may be as simple or as comprehensive as the promoting members wish but there are certain activities such as the supply of alcohol which require specific provisions in the constitution. A form of model constitution that has proved suitable for a number of RYA-affiliated clubs is reprinted at Appendix 2. Although the officers of existing clubs or promoters of new clubs are free to adopt whatever form of constitution they wish, it is worthwhile examining the main headings of the model constitution.

## 1. NAME AND OBJECTS

The objects of a sailing club may be self evident but there will be times when outsiders will want to examine the purposes for which a club has been formed, be it the Regional Sports Council in response to a request for a development grant, a local authority when considering the merits of granting rate relief, or even a civil court when examining a contractual transaction purportedly entered into on behalf of the club. In any of these circumstances a brief declaration of the club's objects will serve to avoid argument and speculation.

## 2.  OFFICERS

While it is conventional for the senior committee members to adopt the style of Commodore, Vice Commodore, Rear Commodore etc. (and even Admiral in the case of some of the most prestigious clubs), there is no need for such titles to be used. It is however a requirement of the Licensing Acts that a members' club which supplies intoxicating liquor to its members shall have a democratically elected management committee, subject to annual re-election. Although the Act does not require officers to stand down permanently after a specific period of service, it will be seen that model Rule 30 provides that, at each AGM, two (of the eight or more) committee members shall stand down and not be eligible for re-election for a further year. This is usually thought desirable to inject new blood into the committee, it being a popular (though not always justified) belief that committee members may go stale after a few years' service and need to be moved on without the option of re-election. Although this can result in the most able and competent committee members being lost to the club, even if only temporarily, there are always means by which they can continue to be involved in club affairs while taking their compulsory sabbatical. Most clubs decide that the rule is desirable, if only to give the chance of painlessly keeping the committee down to size.

Also dealt with under "Officers" are the duties of the Honorary Secretary and Honorary Treasurer. As any Secretary will know, the duties enumerated in the text are but a fraction of those that the typical office holder is likely to have to deal with. Many clubs do not even attempt to lay down his duties, merely providing that the Secretary shall be responsible for administering the affairs of the club. The duties of the Treasurer are easier to define and it is a specific requirement of the Licensing Acts that his duty to prepare annual accounts be covered in the constitution.

## 3.  TRUSTEES

Unless a club has chosen to become incorporated, it cannot hold property itself, since it does not have the necessary separate legal existence for that purpose. Where a club wishes to obtain premises, whether freehold or leasehold, or to have property that is to be enjoyed jointly by the members, some person or persons must therefore accept responsibility for nominal ownership of the property, to be held for the beneficial ownership of the members of the club as a whole.

It is for this purpose that trustees are appointed, usually under terms which oblige them to act in accordance with the directions of the committee. (See Appendix 5 for draft form of bare trust for ownership of a club yacht which can be adopted to cover any form of property). There is no special qualification for a person to act as a trustee save that he should not be a minor and should be in full possession of all his faculties.

Appointment of trustees is made by members in general meeting or by the committee in accordance with the terms of the relevant rule (see model Rule 51) and there should be provision for trustees to resign, or be removed, and for new trustees to be appointed.

Where new trustees are to be appointed, it will be necessary for the old trustees, or the personal representatives of a deceased trustee, to transfer the property to the new trustees. If this is not done then if the club wishes to sell, assign or sub-let the property, the old trustees will first have to be traced in order that a valid transfer can be made.

## 4. MEMBERSHIP

Although a club may provide for as many, or as few, categories of membership as is wished, those most commonly encountered are laid out in the model. Full and family members are those who enjoy the full amenities of the club in return for entry fees and subscriptions. The "lesser" classes of member will usually pay a reduced annual subscription and usually no entry fee. The rules should state when subscriptions are due and payable and provide for termination of membership of defaulters. Although the model rules do not provide that members need be reminded that subscription renewals are due, it may be worthwhile making specific reference if it is not intended that reminders should be sent. It is sometimes thought desirable to specify entry fees and subscriptions in the rules although in practice, to provide flexibility, it is usually more convenient to make this a function of the AGM.

Where trustees hold assets on behalf of the club members generally they may well incur liabilities, in their personal capacities, as legal owners of the property. Nor are they entitled, as of right, to an indemnity from the club members unless this is specifically provided for in the club rules. Model Rule 54 suggests an indemnity from the committee out of the assets of the club which should be sufficient to cover any agreements into which the trustees may enter. It is up to the trustees to ensure they do not undertake obligations which the club funds may be insufficient to cover. Where club funds are likely to fluctuate, and where trustees are contemplating entering into a long-term contract such as for the leasehold of club premises, it may be possible to persuade the other party to agree to limit the trustees' obligations to the amount by which they themselves are entitled to indemnification by the club at the relevant time.

A question that frequently arises in the case of a coastal club (especially one with a good bar and showers) is the admission of visiting yachtsmen. Confusion has been caused by the inclusion of a rule in the model constitution affording admittance to members of any RYA affiliated club. This is included for the benefit of clubs desirous of welcoming bona fide yachtsmen, maximising the use of its facilities, and boosting bar profits without infringing the terms of its licence. It must be stressed that it is for each club to decide what outsiders, if any, will be admitted, or what reciprocal arrangements will be entered into. The fact that such a provision is included in the RYA model constitution should not be taken as an indication that this is an RYA recommendation, let alone a requirement for RYA affiliation.

## 5. MANAGEMENT COMMITTEE

While the constitution may specify a committee of any size or form, in practice between eight and twelve provides a workable body. Less than eight and it will often be impossible to find a quorum, more than twelve and the structure can become unmanageable, not to mention the increased length of time taken by committee meetings. As we have mentioned above, it is a requirement of the Licensing Acts for clubs with a bar that the committee should be elected by the membership to manage the affairs of the club for the stated objects "or for a benevolent or charitable purpose nominated by general meeting".

A convenient procedure for election of members is described in the model constitution, although the club may choose to adopt any style of election. Suffice to say that irregularities, real or imagined, in elective procedures are guaranteed to undermine the stature of even the most respected committee members.

It may be desirable or necessary to provide for ex officio or co-opted committee members either with or without voting rights. In the case of clubs wishing to obtain or maintain registration for the purpose of supplying alcohol, the affairs of the club must be managed (if not by general meeting) by an elective committee. Where ex officio members are given the right to vote, this may disentitle the magistrates from renewing a registration application.

It is normally the function of the Secretary, in concert with the Chairman (or Commodore or President where so termed), to convene meetings, prepare and circulate agenda, deal with minutes and execute decisions of the committee. While it is for the club members to decide on the frequency of committee meetings, it is important for the Secretary to adhere strictly to the rules as to notice, distribution of agenda and so forth, as any committee member aggrieved by a failure to receive notice of a forthcoming meeting (particularly in the event of a deliberate omission) may be entitled to apply to the court for an injunction and a declaration that a decision taken at the meeting was invalid.

## 6.   POWERS OF THE COMMITTEE

It is important (essential in the case of registered clubs) that the committee be given specific powers to manage the club and to enter into contracts and incur liabilities on behalf of the club. Since at common law the ordinary members of the club cannot be made liable for transactions entered into by the committee, unless they knew of and agreed to the transaction, a number of clubs for the peace of mind of the committee members have adopted model Rule 45 which specifically entitles the individual members of the committee to look to the club members (jointly and severally) to cover them against any liability properly incurred by them, up to a sum equal to one year's subscription. The question of liability of officers, committee members and trustees is dealt with more fully in Chapter IV.

Other desirable powers of the committee, to make byelaws governing the behaviour of members and to appoint sub-committees and honorary members, are also dealt with in the model constitution.

## 7.  DISCIPLINING OF MEMBERS

A power that is frequently and necessarily vested in the committee is the enforcement of the rules and the imposition of disciplinary measures including expulsion. For convenience the rules normally give the committee absolute discretion and an expelled member will only succeed in challenging his expulsion in court if he can show that the committee has failed to follow its own rules of procedure, or has acted unfairly in failing to afford him an opportunity of stating his case, or has expelled him for inadequate or irrelevant reasons or in bad faith. A club or committee may only expel a member where the rules specifically provide for such action to be taken.

A member who feels he has been expelled unfairly, unjustly or unconstitutionally will be entitled to seek a declaration from the High Court that the action of the committee was invalid and an injunction restraining the committee or persons acting on their behalf from interfering with his exercise of the rights and privileges that he is entitled to as a member. The court may also award damages, although such an award will usually be made only where the committee's behaviour has been exceptionally bad.

## 8.  BYELAWS

Apart from the formal constitutional provisions in the club rules governing the legal relationship of the members and committee, it is usual for the day-to-day regulations governing behaviour of the members, club facilities and other questions to be dealt with in byelaws. It is for each club to make its own rules but such rules should only be promoted where it is intended to enforce their compliance more or less evenly. An expelled member can always raise the issue of bad faith if he has been singled out unfairly by being expelled for breach of a byelaw which he can show is regularly and consistently ignored by other club members against whom no action has ever been taken. The byelaws laid out in the model are only examples of the sort of rules that the club or committee may wish to adopt. In practice these will vary widely from one club to another dealing typically with standards of dress in various parts of the club at different times, control of animals, parking and mooring of boats and treatment of abandoned boats. This last question is dealt with more fully in Appendix 1 but the statutory rights of the club to deal with old wrecks in the dinghy park and elsewhere on club premises are a lot clearer if the rules specifically provide for certain action to be taken.

## 9. CONDUCT OF MEETINGS

Strict legal principles do not necessarily apply to all club meetings (whether committee meetings or general meetings) but care must be taken to ensure that proceedings are conducted fairly, strictly in accordance with the rules and consistently with established procedures which members may have come to reply upon.

Statutory and customary procedures for company meetings may appear to have little relevance in this context, but in practice it will be found that compliance with such procedures will avoid the sort of disputes which have in the past given rise to costly and time-wasting court proceedings brought by aggrieved members who feel they have been unfairly treated by the club or committee.

### 9.1 Quorum

It is normal for the constitution to specify a quorum for any particular class of meeting and to provide that a meeting shall be abandoned if a quorum is not present within a specified time of the start of the meeting. In the absence of such a rule, any number of members present may elect a chairman and deal with proper business.

### 9.2 Chairman

The constitution should provide for a nominated officer (eg the Commodore) to chair meetings and in the normal course of events it will be for him to take the chair and commence proceedings without formality. In his absence, or if the rules make no specific provision, the first business of the meeting will be the appointment of a chairman for which the person calling the meeting (in most cases the Secretary) will be responsible for inviting nominations. If only one nomination is made, the candidate's name should be voted on and accepted by a majority. If more than one nomination is made, there may be a straight election. Since it is always desirable for a candidate to receive a clear majority, in the case of three or more candidates the rounds of voting should continue with the lowest polling candidate dropping out each time until a clear majority for one candidate is reached.

Once a chairman has been duly elected he may take charge

of the meeting for its full duration, whether or not a vote is taken against him or the permanent chairman arrives in the course of the meeting.

### 9.3 Validity of meeting

The chairman's first duty will be to establish the validity of the meeting, either by himself or the Secretary reading the notice convening it, or by obtaining the agreement of those present to the notice being taken as read. This is an important procedure, for it is the only opportunity for objectors to the validity of the meeting to make their point.

### 9.4 Minutes of previous meeting

If copies of the minutes have previously been circulated before the meeting, those present may agree to have them taken as read. If not, the Secretary should be required to read them. A motion to confirm the minutes should then be taken. The only discussion at this stage should be upon the accuracy of the minutes as a record of what took place at the previous meeting. Any attempt to revise or modify a decision must be ruled out of order by the chairman. When the vote as to the accuracy of the minutes is taken, only persons present at the previous meeting should be entitled to vote.

### 9.5 Matters arising

After confirmation of the previous minutes, there should be the opportunity to discuss relevant questions arising from decisions taken at the previous meeting, but any attempt to change such a decision should not be permitted. Changes to previous resolutions can only be implemented by a properly constituted resolution on the formal agenda of the meeting circulated with the proper notice.

### 9.6 Rights of audience

At large or formal meetings, those wishing to speak should be required to do so on their feet, at the invitation of the chairman only, and shall address all remarks to the chairman. If two members rise to speak at the same time, the chairman should decide which one is to be heard first and the other should sit and wait his turn. Again, in large meetings, it is wise to limit each speaker to one opportunity to speak on each agenda item. Failure to do so can result in difficulties of fair enforcement of the rule over other members.

## 9.7 Resolutions, motions, amendments

Each motion should be clearly and fully formulated in the notice calling the meeting and any changes must be the subject of an equally clearly formulated amendment. For an amendment to be valid it should consist of a qualification of the motion and not merely an expression of disagreement. Matters beyond the scope of the motion which could have been the subject of a separate proposal may not be admitted as amendments. This is particularly important when a meeting is called to alter the rules of a club, since it is manifestly unfair on those who have chosen not to attend a meeting, to find that decisions have been taken on matters which may have been of concern to them. Thus any amendments should be restricted to drafting details. If there are alternative motions, each should appear as a full motion on the agenda.

## 9.8 Proposal of motions

The proposer of a motion should be entiled to speak once to introduce his motion and again at the end of the debate to answer points raised by other speakers, or to deal with proposed amendments. Following that second speech the motion should immediately be put to the meeting and voted upon.

## 9.9 Seconding of motions

A motion must be seconded before any discussion is allowed to take place, either in favour of or against the motion. The seconder of the motion may then speak for the motion or reserve his right until later. If no seconder can be found the motion is lost.

## 9.10 Amendments

An amendment must be proposed and seconded in the same way as an original motion at any time after the motion has been seconded and before the debate has ended, save that the proposer of the amendment does not have the right to reply enjoyed by the proposer of the substantive motion. He may only have one "second" speech and must therefore decide at what stage he wishes to exercise his right of reply, however many amendments are proposed. The same rule of course applies to other speakers who may only speak once, however many amendments are proposed. Each amendment should be dealt with fully before any further amendment is accepted for proposal. If an amendment is carried, it should be put to the meeting in the form of a substantive motion which is then open to further debate and which may itself be made the subject of an amendment. At this stage the mover of the original motion will have the right of making a single speech further to his opening and closing speeches on the main motion. At all times the chairman must have a precise appreciation of the stage which the debate has reached.

### 9.11 Questions

A member who has spoken may, at the discretion of the chairman, put a question to the proposer on a point of clarification but the question should not be allowed to develop into a speech.

### 9.12 Points of order

If a member thinks that there is some defect in the procedure, he may bring it to the chairman at any time and invite the chairman to give a ruling on the question. If the question is raised during another member's speech, the speaker should sit down until the chairman has given his ruling. Only matters of procedure may be the subject of interventions. A contradiction of a misstatement and other means of intervening should not be permitted by the chairman.

### 9.13 Shortening a debate

The chairman under his general power to control the meeting may at any time call a vote on a motion, but should be careful to avoid any risk of apparent prejudice. A motion for a vote may be put at any time by a member who has not previously spoken in the debate, without the need for a seconder. If the closure motion is carried, the chairman should then call on the proposer of the motion to execute his right of reply (if applicable).

### 9.14 Abandonment of debate

An alternative means of ending a debate is a motion "to proceed to the next business". This should only be allowed from a member who has already spoken. The chairman may allow the vote immediately or permit the proposer to explain his motion. No other speech should be allowed on the motion, not even by the proposer of the original motion in exercising his right of reply. If the motion is carried, the meeting passes from the subject under debate to the next agenda item.

## 9.15 Adjournment

A motion for the adjournment of a debate may be proposed at any time, even before the proposer has spoken. The motion should be seconded before a vote can be taken on it. If there is a debate on the adjournment question, the chairman should restrict the substance of speeches to what appears relevant to the question of whether or not the debate should be adjourned. The discussion should not range unnecessarily into the merits of the substantive motion. Amendments must be restricted to the proposed period of adjournment, or to providing for one if the proposer has not dealt with this point. The proposer has no right of reply. If the motion is successful, the chairman will have the right to take the chair at the resumed meeting. Since the later meeting is a continuation of the earlier one, members who have already spoken will not be allowed a further speech.

If the motion for adjournment is lost, the chairman should not accept any further motions for adjournment if he considers they are made simply for the purpose of creating delay.

## 9.16 Disorder

The chairman may declare the meeting adjourned and leave the chair if he thinks the orderly conduct of the meeting is made impossible by members' misbehaviour. Any attempt to continue the proceedings thereafter will be invalid.

## 9.17 Any Other Business

This is an item frequently to be found on agenda papers, but it should not be used as an opportunity for the proposing of a motion that ought to have been the subject of notice to members. Any debate should be limited to a decision to formulate a motion for inclusion as a specific agenda item at a future meeting. At a general meeting this is usually taken as an opportunity for members to air their views and make recommendations to the management committee about the management of the club.

## 9.18 Voting

Unless there are specific rules to the contrary, voting is normally by simple majority by a show of hands. Except for clubs registered under the Licensing Act 1964 which are voting members onto the management committee, the chairman has an extra, casting, vote although he is under no obligation to use it. If voting is equal, then the motion, or the amendment, is lost.

### 9.19 Closing the meeting

If a time limit is reached, the meeting must be closed at that time. Otherwise the meeting comes to a close when the relevant business is concluded, or the meeting is adjourned by resolution, or the chairman in case of disorder. Once the chairman has declared the meeting closed, no further business may be validly transacted.

# II

# INCORPORATION OF A CLUB

## 1. ADVANTAGES AND DISADVANTAGES

In the case of an unincorporated members' club, an individual member can only ever be liable for the payment of his subscription and other sums that may be required from him under the rules (for example an indemnity for trustees and committee members under model Rule 54, Appendix 2). The fact of his membership does not make him personally liable for sums due from the club generally, unless the liability was somehow incurred directly by him or directly on his behalf. Thus committee members or trustees may incur personal liability for contracts entered into on behalf of the club. Although this rarely causes any difficulty, in the case of larger clubs it may sometimes be difficult to find committee members prepared to take on such a risk.

Where that is the case, or where it proves difficult to find trustees willing to hold the club's assets in their names, it may be convenient to consider incorporation under the Companies Acts as an alternative. The Acts provide for companies to be limited by reference either to share capital, as in the case of most commercial undertakings, or by guarantee, which is a very much simpler proposition in the case of a members' club.

Upon incorporation as a company limited by guarantee, the club takes on a separate legal identity and property can be vested in the name of the club rather than in trustees. The club may sue or be sued in its own name and the liability of the members is limited to the guarantee sum (typically £1.00 per member) in the event of a winding-up. However, the expenses of incorporation are greater than the expense of setting up an unincorporated association.

## 2. NAME

The club must obtain clearance from the Registrar of Companies for the proposed name. Clearance will be refused if the name could be confused with that of an existing company or is likely to give a misleading impression of the scale or activities of the undertaking. Nor will the registrar normally permit a name suggesting a connection with the Royal Family such as "King", "Queen", "Royal", "Crown" etc. Thus, if one of the larger yacht clubs with the prefix "Royal" were to seek incorporation, it would be necessary to put to the Registrar a special case for the use of that word before consent would be allowed. The names of sailing clubs which signify an association with a particular town or area will usually be approved by the Registrar. Companies incorporated under the Companies Acts must include, as the last word of their name, the word "Limited", although the Registrar will normally grant a dispensation for companies not intending to trade for profit.

## 3. ARTICLES AND BYELAWS

If a club is incorporated, it will have to include in its constitution the provisions of Table C of the Companies Act 1985, this being the statutory standard form of Articles of Association for a company limited by guarantee. Certain amendments may be made to the standard form of articles, including laying down the requirements for membership, the rights of members, provisions for the holding of general meetings and directors meetings and provisions relating to the constitution and proceedings of the board of directors or council of the company. No alterations may be made to the Articles of Association except at the Annual General Meeting or at an Extraordinary General Meeting specially convenened for that purpose. Accordingly, if a club which is being incorporated has in its constitution or rules certain regulations, for example relating to the running of its club house or premises, it would be advisable to omit these from the Articles and include them in separate byelaws which could be changed by the board of directors from time to time.

## 4. DIRECTORS, MEETINGS AND ACCOUNTS

If a sailing club obtains incorporation under the Companies Acts, the members of the committee will become the directors of the company and will be bound by the relevant provisions of the Acts. For example all new appointments, resignations and changes in particulars must be notified to the Registrar on form 287 within 14 days. All correspondence paper must show the registered number and

16

registered office of the company. Once in every calendar year the club must convene a general meeting to consider and approve the audited accounts, to elect directors who retire by rotation in accordance with the Articles, and to appoint auditors and agree on their remuneration. Special business (such as a proposal to amend the Articles) may also be considered by the AGM provided the necessary notice has been given, the period of notice generally being specified in the Articles. A company must hold an AGM within 18 months of incorporation and not more than 15 months should elapse between AGMs.

Following the AGM an Annual Return (form 363) must be filed with the Registrar within 42 days, accompanied by a set of the final accounts, giving details of mortgages, registered office, and the full composition of the board of directors. A filing fee of £20 should accompany each annual return. Accounts should cover a period not exceeding 18 months, starting from the date of incorporation or the day immediately following the end of the previous accounting period. It should end on the accounting reference date (ARD), or a date up to 7 days either side of the ARD. A company's first accounts should cover a period of more than 6 months.

A company may determine its own ARD within 6 months of incorporation by giving notice to the Registrar on form 224. Otherwise, the ARD will be 31 March. The ARD may be changed by giving notice on form 225(1) (to be delivered before the end of the first accounting reference period to be affected by the change). The accounting reference period cannot be extended to more than 18 months. Accounts should normally be laid before the company and delivered to the Registrar within 10 months of the end of the period covered. If a company's first accounts cover a period of more than 12 months, they must be laid and delivered within 22 months of incorporation. Copies of relevant forms and full Notes for the Guidance of Registered Companies are available free on request from Stationery Section, Companies Registration Office, Crown Way, Cardiff CF4 3UZ. Statutory forms are also available from law stationers.

## 5. LIMITED LIABILITY

Individual members, even those who may have incurred liabilities on behalf of the club, are not liable for the debts of the club unless the company is wound up. Liability will then be limited to the amount of the guarantee. This protection does not extend to directors who have acted fraudulently or recklessly and who may be required to compensate victims of their fraud or recklessness out of their personal assets.

Although the avoidance of personal liability carries obvious attractions for committee members and trustees, in practice few landlords, suppliers or bankers will be willing to enter into potentially onerous contracts, particularly with a small incorporated club, unless the obligations are backed by personal guarantees.

Committee members may often consider incorporation as a means of avoiding liability for accidents occuring to members or visitors on or about the club premises, or in the course of events organised by the club. Legal liability may nonetheless attach to any officer or individual whose negligence has caused damage or injury, irrespective of the legal status of the club. Such risks can most conveniently be faced up to and insured against under the club's own insurance policy for public liability risks.

## 6. THE PROCESS OF INCORPORATION

It is not within the scope of this handbook to give a full account of the process of incorporation. Although it is possible for the lay secretary to undertake the incorporation without professional assistance, in practice it will be very much safer and more convenient to employ a solicitor or a firm of company formation agents to do the work. An "off-the-shelf" company can usually be purchased and the formal steps of incorporation will already have been completed.

Incorporation is a step that should be taken only if, after serious consideration of all the factors involved, it is felt that the benefits outweigh the bureaucratic burden involved in forming and maintaining the company.

# III

# LIABILITY IN CONTRACT AND TORT

## 1. CONTRACTUAL LIABILITY

Members of the committee or trustees of an unincorporated club will be personally liable for contracts with outsiders into which they enter in their own names, unless the other party has specifically agreed to look only to the club funds for payment.

Liability may also be incurred by committee members for the acts of employees appointed by them, in the carrying out of contracts made by the committee. Similarly a committee member who has authorised (and such authorisation can be inferred merely from his presence at a relevant meeting) a servant to give an order to a supplier, can be personally liable for payment. In order to succeed in such a claim, it would be necessary for the creditor to prove authorisation or acquiescence by the individual against whom he is making the claim. If the club steward orders goods without the authority of the committee, even though he may hold himself out as having the necessary authority, the supplier will only be entitled to claim reimbursement from the members of the committee if he can prove that they were privy to the contract by individually authorising it, or that the dealing on credit was for the furtherance of the purposes and objects of the club.

It is not open to the committee or club employees to pledge the credit of club members without specific authority. The committee has authority only to manage accumulated subscriptions and thus any proposed mortgage or long-term liability should be put to the members for approval at a general meeting unless specifically provided for in the club rules.

It follows that the ordinary member does not incur personal liability for goods obtained by the club, unless provided for in the club rules. If a creditor wishes to enforce payment by legal action, he cannot simply commence proceedings against the club, but must seek out an individual member or members of the committee as defendants. This does not apply where goods are ordered by the club for the benefit of individual members; in such circumstances the members will incur personal liability.

## 2.  TORTIOUS LIABILITY

A tort is a civil wrong, arising from a breach of duty other than under contract, leading to liability for damages or injunction. Tortious liability in this context arises most commonly from negligence and nuisance, and to a lesser extent where a sailing club or school may be concerned, from trespass and libel.

The major causes of liability to the public and other club members are examined in detail in Chapter IV. We will consider here the circumstances in which club officers, trustees and members may find themselves in a position of potential liability.

The principle upon which club members' liability is founded is that if a wrongful act is done by a servant or agent, the employer or principal is liable if the act is done with the principal's express or implied authority, or in the course of employment. Accordingly, the tortious act of a club steward of an incorporated club acting in his official capacity will almost inevitably render the company vicariously liable. In the case of an unincorporated club, the injured party would have to prove that the steward was acting as agent of the members of the club or committee. The fact that the steward was performing (however badly) the sort of function for which he was employed will normally be sufficient to establish vicarious liability.

When trustees hold premises on behalf of the members of an unincorporated club the law attaches to them all the liabilities of ownership. Liability for injury caused to a visitor, under the Occupiers Liability Act 1957 (see below), is likely to attach jointly to the members of the club who can be considered as occupiers to the same extent as the trustees.

Liability will not rest equally on all members. If for example a club member is injured he cannot sue the other members in their capacity as members, since they do not owe him any duty to ensure that the premises were safe; as a member of the club he cannot claim to be a visitor.

## 3. OCCUPIERS' LIABILITY

Liability for damage caused by the structural condition of the premises onto which persons may come may exist as between the committee and club members, or as between the club generally and visitors. There may also be liability for personal injury or damage due to the defective state of the premises towards a person who might reasonably be expected to be affected by those defects, or against a landlord who has let the premises to a club (incorporated or unincorporated) if he is under an obligation to the tenant to maintain or repair.

In so far as the club is the occupier of premises, Section 2(1) of the Occupiers' Liability Act 1957 imposes on the members as a whole, or on the company in the case of an incorporated club, a "common duty of care" towards all visitors. This is defined by the Act as a duty "to take such care as in all the circumstances of the case is reasonable to see that the visitor will be reasonably safe in using the premises for the purposes for which he is invited by the occupier to be there ". The Act recognises that the occupier may be "free to . . . . extend, restrict, modify or exclude that duty to any visitor or visitors by agreement or otherwise".

An occupier's duty of care may be modified in a number of ways including by giving a clear warning of potential danger to the visitor, so long as that warning, if heeded, would be enough to make the visitor reasonably safe. The visitor may also be bound by the terms of an exclusion clause in the contract, although such clauses, since the Unfair Contract Terms Act 1977, will only operate to protect the club if the term was reasonable in all the circumstances. Also relevant as a potential defence is the maxim *volenti non fit injuria*. To rely on this principle the defendant (i.e. the club) must obtain a finding of fact by the court that the plaintiff voluntarily and freely, with full knowledge of the nature of the risk, impliedly agreed to incur it. Even a young person may be deemed to have consented to the risk of injury by participating in a game or sport.

Liability from other sources, such as participation in yacht races, is dealt with more fully in Chapter IV.

## 4. LITIGATION

If a club is incorporated, it has the legal capacity to sue or to be sued. An unincorporated club, on the other hand, does not have that capacity and only individuals associated with

21

the club, whether trustees, committee members or ordinary members, may take action. Clearly individuals associated with a club can be sued individually, but a plaintiff wishing to take action against the members as a whole must take a representative action against named defendants. High Court procedural rules specify that "where numerous persons have the same interest in any proceedings, the proceedings may be begun by or against any one or more of them as representing all, or one or more of them". This rule is designed to establish a right against a fund, rather than to enforce a personal liability.

If the proposed action involves club property vested in the trustees, the trustees are the proper persons to sue and be sued in that respect. The court may however, at any stage of the proceedings, order the members of the club or some of them to be added or substituted as parties. Whether or not such an order is made, any judgement against the trustees is binding on the beneficiaries so long as the trustees have been representing their interests.

The court may award not only damages, but an injunction, in appropriate circumstances. An injunction in a representative action will be valid and enforceable against all members of an unincorporated association. An injunction will only be granted if the injury is of such a character that the plaintiff can not practically be compensated by damages.

# IV

# POTENTIAL LIABILITY
# TO THIRD PARTIES

As indicated in Chapter III a yacht club can incur civil liability for a number of reasons. We are here concerned with the possible legal liability of a yacht club as a result of things done (or not done) in the course of its normal activities, especially organising yacht races, and ancillary activities such as launching vessels and providing escort and rescue services.

In most cases it is not difficult to recognise where a yacht club has committed a breach of contract. If however a club is sued for something that has happened in the course of a yacht race, tortious liability may have arisen and the position will be less clear. In most cases the plaintiff will allege that the cause of the injury or damage was the negligence of the club.

Negligence can be described as either the carrying out of any act which a reasonable man would not have carried out, or the failure to do something which a reasonable man would have done. The "reasonable man" test is used by the law to determine what standards persons must live up to when carrying out those activities which affect others.

Not every act of negligence will give a person injured by it a legal right to compensation. In order to support an action for negligence, the injured person must show that he has been injured as a result of a duty owed to him by the negligent person to avoid injuring him. Such a legal duty is owed to those persons who ought to be foreseen as likely to be affected by the act or omission in question. It is often unclear precisely what degree of relationship will give rise on the one side to a duty to take care and on the other side to a right to expect that care will be taken.

It may not be readily apparent which particular circumstances give rise to legal duties, thereby requiring a yacht club to take care to avoid inflicting injury by negligence. The court will examine the merits of every new set of circumstances. A plaintiff need not bring the facts of any situation within those of previous cases in which a duty of care has been held to exist. It is irrelevant that a particular set of circumstances is novel or has never been before a court in the past. The court is always ready to recognise a new legal duty.

A court examining the problem would probably seek guidance from the following:

(a) What classes of persons are likely to be affected by the activities of a yacht club.
(b) What a reasonable yacht club of similar size and with similar facilities would do in similar circumstances.
(c) What the normally accepted activities of yacht clubs are and what the precise scope of organising a race appears to be.
(d) What standards the particular yacht club, and other yacht clubs, maintain.

A person who succeeds in proving that a yacht club's conduct was negligent (i.e. in breach of a duty of care) will then have to prove that the negligence actually caused the injury or damage. Should he do so, he will be entitled to damages.

Certain defences may be open to the yacht club. These are described in more detail later in this chapter, but in brief it may be alleged that:

(a) The club's negligence/breach of duty did not cause the injury or damage.
(b) The injured person willingly and voluntarily accepted the risk of injury. In legal terms this defence is expressed by the Latin phrase *volenti non fit injuria*. This is a complete defence if established, but it cannot apply to an injured child of an age at which he is deemed to be incapable of making a judgement as to his own safety. This age will vary from one child to another and according to the circumstances of the case but the defence of *volenti* will generally not apply to a young person of 13 years or less.
(c) The injured person was contributorily negligent in failing to take care for his own safety. Where contributory negligence is established the court will reduce the damages to which the injured person is otherwise entitled by such amount as it thinks fit.

Most clubs are associations of persons and are not incorporated as limited companies. In such an association the members themselves form the club as a body. The law does not permit a member to sue his own club for negligence unless his injury was due to some officer of the club exceeding his authority or carrying out his duties in such a grossly negligent manner that an excess of authority can be implied.

A number of clubs are incorporated as limited companies and others are proprietary clubs where someone who owns certain premises and facilities admits people who pay their subscriptions to make use of them. The owners will run such a club with a view to profit. Where such incorporated or proprietary clubs are concerned, they can be sued in negligence by the members.

## 1. CLUB AS ORGANISER OF YACHT RACES

For this purpose the persons who are likely to be affected by the activities of the yacht club can be divided into three classes:

(a) The competitor — the actual person who enters a yacht for a race. This will normally be the owner of the yacht;
(b) Crew members;
(c) Third parties.

Of prime concern will be the possible liability of the organising club to these persons in negligence. The competitor, since he makes a contract with the club on entering the race, will also have certain contractual rights.

### 1.1 Liability in negligence to competitors

Before attempting to predict how far a club's liability in negligence may extend, the scope of the activity of organising a yacht race must be clarified.

Firstly, there are the basic aspects such as laying the course, determining the classes of entrants, starting and finishing the race, determining the final positions and awarding prizes. Secondly, a set of rules will be provided to govern the event. The rules may contain undertakings on the part of the club which might give rise to liability in contract. In the context of negligence the rules will provide a useful guide to establish the general parameters of yacht race organisation. Where the rules are those that are generally accepted as an integral part of yacht race organisation — such as the International Yacht Racing Rules — then any club adhering to them will not be seriously at risk. However, non-adherence could result in liability in negligence. Thirdly, a particular club may have consistently kept to certain standards. The club may thus be obliged to exercise reasonable care in maintaining those

25

standards and may be liable if it negligently fails to do so.

With these factors in mind, certain specific aspects of the organisation of a yacht race can now be considered:

### 1.1.1 *Laying the course*

A negligently laid course could well cause harm to the competitors taking part in the race. For example if a mark were placed too close to a dangerous shoal or some other hazard, causing a competitor or his craft to sustain injury, then the club might be liable in damages.

The race rules will usually cover the eventuality of a mark which has shifted or gone missing. IYR Rule 9 is such a rule and provides that the race committee shall "when possible" replace or substitute the mark, or substitute for it a buoy or vessel displaying the International Code Flag "M" — the Mark signal. The rule goes on to state that should any of these options be impossible, the race committee may, at its discretion, cancel or abandon the race or shorten the course.

Such a rule may well lead a court to find as a fact that dealing with marks which have shifted or gone missing is an accepted part of yacht race organisation. As a result, negligent replacement or substitution, or even doing nothing, could amount to negligence, for example if a mark had drifted into a perilous position. The words "when possible" do not provide a complete escape for a yacht club. The decision as to whether any action is or is not possible would have to be taken reasonably. The absence of an available vessel to take necessary action would not necessarily be a valid reason, although physical impossibility due to bad weather would be. If replacement or substitution is not possible where the absence or shifting of the mark has created a situation of danger, the committee ought to abandon the race or shorten the course.

### 1.1.2 *Racing in foul weather*

The choice of a course, the timing of a racing event and the decision whether to start the race at all or whether to allow a race in progress to continue, are all decisions which will be influenced by the weather. Also relevant will be the type of race, the size of the vessels and the competence of competitors. Whatever decision is eventually arrived at, it ought to be made on the best information available. In certain circumstances, starting a race when gale force winds are known to be imminent could amount to lack of due care for competitors and thus negligence in law.

### 1.1.3 *Provision of safety equipment*

Most rules governing yacht racing firmly lay the responsibility for providing adequate life safety equipment upon the competitors themselves (eg. IYR Rule 24). However, racing rules may give a club discretion to inspect vessels to ensure that they are adequately provided with proper gear. A United States Court decided in 1974 that a yacht club was under no legal duty to inspect life saving equipment in circumstances where the race was run in accordance with "well established rules".

Clubs do not have to guarantee their races safe, but do have the responsibility to decide what, if any, safety regulations are appropriate (having regard to the type of yacht, type of water sailed, anticipated weather and sea conditions, experience and ability of skippers and crews etc).

The individual clubs are, and must remain, the best judges as to what safety procedures and regulations, if any, should be laid down and enforced. The RYA cannot prescribe one set of rules suitable for all.

The regulations used will to some extent be controlled by the resources available for enforcement. A club with limited resources reliant on inexperienced race officers, but with an experienced sailing adult membership, should not undertake or try to enforce exhaustive safety regulations. A club with competent race officers and a substantial number of novices or young sailors would be wise at least to carry out spot checks or impose a self-checking questionnaire upon competitors.

Take two contrasting examples:

(a) A small inland sailing club with few resources catering for experienced sailors in summer only, on a small area of water, may have a case for imposing no safety rules whatever, on the basis that competitors may decide for themselves what is sensible. An accident under these circumstances should only bring blame on a club or race officer if there was some positive act which caused the accident.

(b) A large well funded organisation running races in which competitors have to be self-sufficient and self-reliant for extended periods (eg the Round the World Race) or where

27

there is a likelihood of inexperienced sailors joining crews, would be wise to impose comprehensive safety requirements in particular for the benefit of crew members who may be at increased risk if yachts are not built or equipped to required standards.

## Dinghy and small keelboat races

A club may for example decide that, during certain times of the year, personal buoyancy and protective clothing shall be worn. The club may lay down a policy on the number and operating method of any safety boats. These procedures, if adopted, should be consistently enforced and adhered to.

## Offshore races

Clubs organising races offshore should consider using the appropriate ORC Special Regulations Governing Minimum Equipment and Accommodation Standards (ORC: 19 St James's Place, London SW1A 1NN), and should consider the self- checking forms used by the RORC (20 St James's Place, London SW1A 1NN).

## CHS advisory numbers

Yachts rated under the Channel Handicap System (CHS) are now given rating certificates with 'advisory numbers' to indicate suitability for various kinds of racing. Clubs should consider establishing a method by which the minimum safety number appropriate to the race is published to competitors.

## Novices

A novice may not be aware of the implications of particular conditions and may not know of deficiencies in the equipment or the boat. Race committees must bear this in mind in organising events.

## Appropriate action in changing weather conditions

Changes in weather are publicly forecast and weather and sea state changes are often a contributory cause to casualties. When deteriorating weather conditions could cause an organising club to, for example, shorten or abandon a race (if that is part of the club's understood method of working) the club must monitor, as far as reasonably practicable, the weather and weather forecasts. The Committee should be prepared to take appropriate action.

## Consistent and competent application

Whatever system is adopted must be applied consistently

and competently. Failure to apply an established system, or the negligent carrying out of inspection checks, could impose liability on the club.

### 1.1.4  *System of inspection*

Where safety regulations exist, the yacht owner will warrant compliance when signing the entry form. This will protect the club from any claim from him arising from his own non-compliance.

The problem arises with crew members who have no contractual relationship with the club. If injured by reason of a breach in the safety requirements, they might argue that they were entitled to rely on the club carrying out some system of inspection since this is now such a common practice. A club may find it difficult to argue, depending on the nature of the event and the resources of the club, that no inspection at all was necessary. The club's duty would be discharged by taking reasonable steps to ensure that yachts comply, the level of reasonableness being dependent on the type of racing organised by the club. A system of consistently applied spot checks would probably be reasonable.

If it can be shown by a plaintiff crew member that the club did not take reasonable steps to enforce its own rules, liability might be established. In such circumstances the club should be able to claim an indemnity from the owner of the yacht in respect of any damages.

### 1.1.5  *Provision of escorts and/or patrol craft*

Clubs will not normally be under any legal duty to provide such services. Yacht racing rules do not generally contain any provision for escorts or patrol craft and this confirms the absence of any such legal duty.

If it is the custom of a particular club to provide patrol craft and escorts, different considerations may apply. The courts may take the view that the competitors are reasonably entitled to rely on such a service if it is customary to provide it.

### 1.1.6  *Seaworthiness of competing yachts*

A race committee which believes that a particular boat is unseaworthy, either because of defects in the boat or its gear or because it is unsafe in the prevailing or expected conditions, may be under an obligation at least to warn both skipper and crew.

29

If an entry in a potentially arduous race is crewed by young people or novices a race committee should consider carefully whether it should be refused entry in the race. Power to do this is given in IYR Rule 1.3 "the organising authority or the race committee may, before the start of a race or series, reject or rescind the entry of any yacht or exclude a competitor, without stating the reason".

Such an obligation would only arise when the club has knowledge of the deficiency. Each club must make up its own mind whether it should institute a system for assessing the seaworthiness of craft and/or the experience and ability of skippers and crews.

As a general rule, race organisers should avoid becoming too involved with the stability of competitors' yachts. The more they do so the greater the likelihood of being found negligent if something is missed on inspection, or if the club fails to notify the owner that an inadequate stability ratio has been discovered in the measurement figures. Where, however, a specific fault on a specific boat or class of boat comes to the notice of the organising club, it cannot avoid taking account of this and ensuring that their rules cover the situation.

### 1.1.7 *Competence of competitors and their crew*

A competitor taking part in a race will in most circumstances voluntarily assume the risk that other competitors may be less experienced and competent than himself. Indeed he will be hoping to show this by winning the race!

A United States Court has ruled that a yacht club is under no legal duty to ensure that competitors are competent. That, however, may not be the case where an obviously incompetent individual was allowed to compete in a race, even if the rules of the race make no mention of competitors' competence. Particular events may have special rules governing them. Such rules may provide for checks or tests to establish a competitor's ability. The existence of such rules may give rise to a legal duty on the part of the club to exclude incompetent persons from taking part in the race.

### Children and young persons

Different considerations arise where children and young persons are concerned. A child will never be held by a court to have voluntarily assumed a risk, unless he is of sufficient age and intelligence to appreciate the risk in question.

In situations where a club is already under a duty to exercise care to avoid injuring adults by negligence, it will be under a duty of a higher standard towards children. Even if in some given situation no duty at all would rest upon the club to exercise care towards adults, children in a similar situation may nonetheless be entitled to claim a degree of care from the club.

### Inexperienced competitors

Clubs which organise races and advertise widely for entrants should bear in mind that the steady growth in popularity of the sport, and the increasing encouragement of less experienced people to take part in competitive yachting, inevitably imposes a high duty on a yacht club or organising committee to take reasonable steps to ensure that their events are reasonably safe for all who participate.

Particularly in the case of sail training races, young and inexperienced trainees between the ages of 15 and 25, often responding to public advertisements in the press by commercial or quasi-commercial operators, are those most at risk. The organisers of such races may owe a duty of care to each participant to provide a "safe framework" for the race. Such a framework would include such matters as the course, the weather, the safety equipment to be carried, communications, emergency procedures, bringing seaworthiness and safety matters to the attention of participants and seeking to ensure that the race rules are obeyed. Whether the courts would, in fact, expect such a high standard of care to be exercised by a Race Committee is yet to be tested.

## 1.2 Defences to negligence

### 1.2.1 *Volenti non fit injuria*

A person cannot be heard to complain of injury or damage if he voluntarily accepts the risk of such injury or damage. Thus a competitor in a yacht race may reasonably be assumed to accept the following risks:

(a) The risk of racing without proper life saving equipment;
(b) The ordinary perils of the sea including adverse weather;
(c) The risk that other competitors will not be as competent, though not substantially less competent, as he himself is;
(d) The risk of racing in an unseaworthy vessel;

31

(e)  The risk of using an inexperienced crew; and

(f)  The risk of sailing in an area he knows to be unsafe.

As we have seen, this defence is not available where a child of, say, 13 or less has been injured, or where a complete novice is involved.

### 1.2.2  *Negligence not causing damage*

He who complains of injury or damage must prove that the yacht club's negligence/breach of duty actually caused the injury or damage, or at least materially contributed to it.

### 1.2.3  *Contributory negligence*

Failure to take care of one's own safety can cause the injured person to have his amount of damages reduced, by whatever amount the court thinks fit. This can be by a factor of anything from a 10% reduction in damages to 90%.

### 1.3  **Contractual liability**

When entering a race a competitor enters into a contract with the organising club and is deemed to agree to and be bound by the rules which govern the race. Specific undertakings made by the club in these rules or a race invitation will form part of the contract. A club may be liable if any of the undertakings are breached. An unincorporated club is not liable to its own members in negligence but will be liable to them for breach of contract. It is prudent for a yacht club to keep its undertakings to a minimum and avoid promising to provide escort craft or to inspect vessels for safety equipment and seaworthiness or to check insurance certificates for validity or competitors for competence. The club should make it a condition of entry that safety equipment, seaworthiness, insurance etc. are matters entirely for the owners. (See also Appendix 11 on the inspection of insurance documents).

Contracts may contain terms which seek to limit or exclude one party's liability. A great deal of law relating to such terms exists — culminating in the Unfair Contract Terms Act 1977. These aspects are considered below.

### 1.4  **Defence to contractual liability**

Any competitor suing a yacht club for a breach of contract must prove that it was the club's breach which caused the injury or damage complained of. If the damage or injury was caused by some other act or omission the club will not be liable.

If the injured person has failed to take care for his own safety, it is not entirely clear whether the law will reduce his damages by reason of his contributory negligence. Certainly if the club's breach of contract was caused by the injured person's negligence the amount of damages will be reduced.

## 1.5 Liability to crew of competing craft

A crew member has no contractual rights against the yacht club organising the race, unless perhaps all of those crewing a yacht have entered as a team. An aggrieved crew member would have to prove that the club was negligent in some way, and what was said above about duties of care owed to competitors would also apply in relation to their crew. Defences open to the club may be limited in relation to crew members. Such a person is less likely to be contributorily negligent, because for example he may not know that the vessel is unseaworthy. A club will not be able to claim that a crew member has voluntarily accepted a risk if the crew member knew of the risk but did not accept it, for example if he protested about the owner taking a risk but had no choice but to stay on board and suffer the risk.

## 1.6 Liability to third parties

The ambit of the law of negligence is wide and expanding. It is possible that a club will incur tortious liability towards persons who have no connection with the race or the club but who are injured or who suffer loss due to the negligent organisation of the race.

For example, a third party may have a valid claim against a competitor and the club where the club laid a race through an area where many vessels were moored, causing damage to a moored vessel by a competing yacht. It is unlikely that a third party would have a claim against a club for damage suffered as a result of a competing yacht being unseaworthy, seaworthiness being the sole responsibility of the owner.

## 1.7 Joint negligence

Where the yacht club organising a race is negligent and damage is suffered by someone, the damage may also have been caused as a result of the negligence of another person. Take the case of a crew member who is injured as a result of the club's negligent organisation and the owner's negligent navigation. In such a case, if the club paid for the whole of the damage, it could seek to recover a contribution from the owner. The amount of contribution would be such as the court finds just and equitable.

## 2. OTHER SOURCES OF LIABILITY

### 2.1 Launching vessels

Launching vessels is an activity in which a yacht club may from time to time engage. If not carried out in a proper manner, a club might incur liability, for example if it managed the launching in a negligent manner or if the physical condition of the slipway was not of a proper standard.

### 2.2 Organising escorts, rescue etc.

Escort and rescue vessels must be navigated and managed in a proper manner, although in cases of emergency there may be some excuse for say, proceeding at an excessive speed. Where the club owns the vessels, it stands in the same position as any other owner. If some other person's boat is borrowed by the club, the club will be responsible for the safe navigation of the boat if an officer of the club is in charge. Where the borrowed vessel remains under the control of its owner, the club may find itself liable, under the law of agency, for the owner's negligence.

Vessels and personnel appointed for escort or rescue operations should be suitable and capable. However, where the owner of the vessel "volunteers" himself and the vessel, rather than being requested to help by the club, the club is not likely to be liable for the owner's negligence, unless if could be said that he acts as agent on behalf of the club. Agency can arise from express words used, such as "I am carrying out this service for the club", or from the circumstances. For example:

(a) Could the club be said to have a legal duty to provide escort or rescue services (perhaps because of a custom or contract or because the competitors are young children)? If so, then an agency situation may arise.

(b) Did the club's negligence create the danger which required the provision of a rescue service? If so, the person who undertakes the rescue may well subsequently allege he was doing it for the club's benefit, although this was never expressly requested. Where the owner of the vessel who offers his services himself suffers injury or damage, then if he can prove he was acting as the club's agent, he will be entitled to reimbursement by the club. The club will not be liable for the agent's loss or damage caused by his own negligence.

## 2.3  Team races

Where a team is racing on behalf of the club it is doubtful if the club are responsible for the team's acts or omissions. If the club owns the boats it will have some obligation to take care, since the team can be said to be acting as the club's agents. Where the team consists of young children, the club might well be responsible. A negligent team of children using a boat would probably render the club liable.

## 2.4  Crew registers

If a club organises such a facility it should protect itself from potential liability in the event of a crew member being injured while on board a yacht to which he was introduced by the register. The club should establish its position as agent of the owner rather than as an independent body warranting the seaworthiness of the yacht or competence of the crew. This should be done by notice to the potential crew member on accepting his or her name for the register stating that the club acts as the agent of the owner. The club is thereby disclosing the agency and impliedly absolving itself from liability.

## 3.  EXCLUSION AND EXEMPTION CLAUSES

Such clauses are all now subject to the provisions of the Unfair Contract Terms Act 1977. This Act applies to clauses in a contract or in a notice given to persons generally (i.e. a notice contained in a contract given to the world at large). The Act places restrictions on the use of such clauses and notices where they seek to exclude liability for breach of obligations or duties arising:

(a) from things done or to be done in the course of a business; or

(b) from the occupation of premises used for the business purposes of the occupier.

Can a yacht club which organises yacht races be said to be carrying on a business? If the club is a proprietary club it will in all probability be held to be carrying on a business. The position of unincorporated and incorporated members' clubs is less certain; the meaning of "business" will vary from circumstance to circumstance. Intention to make a profit will be evidence that a club is carrying on a business, although profit is not necessary. At least part of every yacht club's activities, such as providing a bar and dining facilities, will come within the scope of carrying on a business.

Recent case law on tax questions indicates it is no longer safe to assume that, just because the participants and organisers are drawn together by love of the sport rather than a commercial motive, the activity is not to be regarded as a business. Thus it is likely that aspects of the race organisation to be regarded as "business-like" activity would include: making a surplus in order to defray other expenses of the club and to subsidise the subscriptions of members; advertising to non-members and holding numerous open meetings; and the sale of associated regalia such as badges, T-shirts etc. to the public.

Even where an exclusion clause or notice is not covered by the Act, or for some reason does not offend against the Act (see below), it may still not be effective. The courts dislike exclusion clauses and have laid down strict rules for their application. The clause or notice must not be ambiguous. It must be clear enough to cover the type of liability in question and it must be brought to the notice of the other party (eg. the competitor). The other party need not have actual notice of it; reasonable steps to bring it to his attention will be sufficient.

The competitor entering into a contract with the club should be referred to any exclusion clauses by the document which he signs, especially if they are not contained in the same document. Where the exclusion clauses are contained in the rules governing the race, then if the rules are well established the competitor will be taken to know of them, as any sportsman would know the rules of his particular sport.

Any liability to the crew of a yacht who have no contractual relationship with the club could be excluded by a general notice posted in a conspicuous place where it can be reasonably seen or by proof that they knew of the special rules which may include provisions excluding liability.

In the case of a proprietary club, or some other type of club which organises yacht races with a prime view to profit rather than the promotion of the sport, the Act will almost certainly apply and liability for death or personal injury caused by negligence cannot be excluded. In the case of other loss or damage, liability cannot be excluded unless the clause or notice satisfies the test of reasonableness. Matters such as the bargaining strength of the parties, and whether the injured party knew of the clause or notice, are to be used as guidelines.

In the case of occupier's liability the Act applies when the occupier's premises are occupied for the purpose of a business, for example dining or drinking. Otherwise a notice seeking to exclude liability will not achieve its purpose unless in all the circumstances the premises enable the visitor to be reasonably safe.

Rules such as the IYR Rules do not appear to offend the Act. The parts in the rules about laying marks, provision of information about tides and weather, choosing courses etc. could give rise to liability. Indeed, it may not be thought desirable to seek to exclude such liability. The yacht club can always protect itself by insurance. It is undesirable to adopt a legalistic approach to those tasks that a yacht club will usually perform in the course of organising a race. On the other hand, exclusion of liability is probably desirable to protect the club from consequences arising from matters beyond its control — such as seaworthiness of vessels and the provision of life safety equipment on yachts. The IYR rules adequately achieve this purpose.

Two important points arise:

By Section 4(1) of the Act "A person dealing as a consumer cannot by reference to any contract term be made to indemnify another person (whether a party to the contract or not) in respect of liability that may be incurred by the other for negligence or breach of contract, except in so far as the contract term satisfies the requirement of reasonableness". Thus, while an exclusion clause on its own will probably be invalid it is not clear that an indemnity clause will necessarily be invalid.

By Section 11(1) "... the requirement of reasonableness ... is that the term shall have been a fair and reasonable one to be included having regard to the circumstances which were, or ought reasonably to have been, known to or in the contemplation of the parties when the contract was made".

It is necessary to look at the circumstances surrounding the

37

entry of a yacht in a race and ask whether it would be reasonable for the owner to be responsible for any loss, damage, death or personal injury as a result of taking part in the race, howsoever caused. This would probably not be unreasonable, especially against a background where if the yacht was unseaworthy or poorly navigated the owner would probably have to indemnify the organising club anyway (as discussed above).

In view of the current uncertainty in the law it is advisable that the declaration on the entry form should include both exclusion and indemnity clauses. It may be that one or both could be rendered invalid by the operation of the Act. Furthermore Section 2(3) states "Where a contract term or notice purports to exclude or restrict liability for negligence, a person's agreement to or awareness of it is not of itself to be taken as indicating his voluntary acceptance of any risk." Thus, the knowledge of the existence of an exclusion clause, even if invalid, would have some value in helping to prove an awareness on the part of an owner of the risks involved in yacht racing, although further evidence of full appreciation and acceptance of those risks would be necessary. Not only should the exclusion and indemnity clauses be on the entry form (where probably only the owner would see them) but they should be prominently displayed on the race instructions and on any other suitable literature, to ensure the widest possible circulation amongst owners and their crews.

Another way of seeking to bind crew members contractually to the terms and conditions of the entry form (which is normally only signed by the owner or skipper) is to treat the owner as agent by making him acknowledge that he is signing the entry form for himself and on behalf of his skipper and crew, and that he warrants that he has authority to do so. If a crew member then subsequently makes a claim against the organising club and alleges that the owner had no authority to sign the entry form on his behalf, the organising club can implead the owner in contract for breach of his warranty of authority.

## 3.1  Children and Juniors

Persons under the age of 18 are unable to bind themselves in contract, except for the provision of "necessaries (i.e. food, clothing, education etc.) and in the context of yacht racing an exclusion clause will not be binding on a minor.

Even where a disclaimer is signed by a parent or guardian this will only disentitle the parents from making a claim in the event of an accident and will not affect the child's legal rights.

## 4. LIMITATION OF LIABILITY

An important provision, of particular relevance to some of a yacht club's possible liabilities, is the law which states that a shipowner or dockowner can limit his liability towards persons suffering loss or damage, due to negligent navigation of his ship or management of his dock as the case may be.

### 4.1 Launching

The Merchant Shipping (Liability of Shipowners and Others) Act 1900 provides that the owners of a dock will not be liable for damage beyond the amount that would be payable by the largest registered British ship visiting the dock over the previous five years, subject to a minimum of 166,667 Units of Account for death or physical injury or 83,333 Units for property damage (a Unit of of Account being approximately 80p in 1987).

To benefit from the provisions of the Act, certain conditions must be satisfied:

(a) The club must be the owner or occupier of a "dock" which is defined by the Act to include "slips, quays, wharves, piers, landing places and jetties". All yacht clubs will probably satisfy this condition.

(b) The damage must occur within an area over which the owner of the "dock" exercises control. If there is an enclosed dock this area is easily ascertained. Where the usual sort of slipway is concerned such area will probably include the slipway itself plus a little of the area beyond which must be kept clear if the slipway is to be of any use.

(c) The damage must take place without the actual fault or privity of the club. Fault of the club's employees or agents does not constitute actual fault or privity. What will amount to actual fault or privity is the fault of those who authorised the launching, for example a committee or, in the case of an incorporated club, the directors or other officers, or in the case of a proprietary club, the owner. Those persons who take the benefit of limited liability ought to take all reasonable steps to ensure that the launching is carried out safely and in accordance with the law and that persons working at the launching are

39

competent.

## 4.2  Merchant Shipping Acts 1894/1979

Under the Merchant Shipping Acts 1894 to 1979 the owners, charterers, managers or operators of a ship can limit their liability unless it is proved that the loss resulted from a personal act or omission committed with intent to cause such loss, or recklessly and with knowledge that such loss would result. The following categories of loss are included under the Act:

(a) Loss of life or personal injury caused to any person being carried on the ship;

(b) Damage to property on board the ship; and

(c) Loss of life or personal injury caused to any person not carried on the ship, through the act or omission of any person (whether on board the ship or not) in the navigation or management of the ship . . . or through any act or omission of any persons on board the ship.

Laying up and launching would appear to come within the definition of "navigation or management". For property damage, insurers will not be able to limit an owner's liability below 83,333 Units of Account (see above). For loss of life or personal injury the level will be 166,667 Units. (Merchant Shipping Act 1979 ss 17-19 and Sch. 4-5).

## 4.3  Occupiers' liability

The possible liability of a yacht club for the dangerous condition of slipways, jetties etc. and seabed has already been mentioned. Where damage is caused by reason of such dangerous condition, the club may limit liability under the Merchant Shipping (Liability of Shipowners and Others) Act 1900. The damage must be caused without the actual fault or privity of the club. The limitation figure would be as described above.

Occupier's liability extends to ships as well as land and buildings. Vessels "occupied" by the club must be in such a condition that a visitor is reasonably safe. Under the Merchant Shipping Acts liability may be limited in respect of injury or damage to persons or property carried in a ship, where the injury or damage is caused without the actual fault or privity of the yacht club.

## 4.4   Escort and rescue craft

In respect of damage caused by such vessels, a yacht club may limit its liability under the Merchant Shipping Acts should the vessel be owned, chartered, etc. by the club, or if the club has an interest in it, and if damage is caused without the actual fault or privity of the club. Problems may arise where the club borrows a vessel for escort and rescue work and the owner of the vessel continues to navigate. Payment of a fee for the use of the vessel could enable the yacht club to argue that it had chartered the vessel. Otherwise, the club would find it hard to argue that it was "in possession" of the vessel. Where such vessels are used for this type of activity and are not navigated by a club representative, care should be taken to ensure that the person in charge of the vessel is experienced and capable. Liability could befall the club if the escort or rescue craft was damaged or caused damage, as the owner could be said to be an agent of the club.

## 4.5   Duties in organising races

For faults in the laying of the course, laying of markers etc. limitation of liability is not possible.

# V

# INSURANCE

Throughout the previous chapter on public liability, much emphasis has been laid on the importance of adequate third party insurance arrangements for clubs and club officers.

The standard RYA club insurance policy provides for cover under ten separate heads:

## 1. BUILDINGS

As with house or commercial premises insurance, it is important in proposing building insurance to define exactly what property is to be covered and against precisely what risks. Underwriters frequently entitle their cover "All Risks" when in fact what they mean is "Some Risks", the term referring to risks of direct accidental physical loss or damage, normally with numerous exclusions. The fundamental concept is that damage must be accidental (or malicious) damage rather than damage arising from wear and tear, encroachment or gradual weathering or erosion. Fabric maintenance tends to fall into arrears from time to time and claims are often made on insurance policies for damage that is in fact delayed maintenance. In these circumstances the underwriter will often be reluctant to pay.

It is worthwhile giving thought to the sort of incidents that can occur. For instance, could a high tide coupled with high winds cause damage to dinghy or car park surfaces or retaining walls? Are all dinghy ramps, slipways etc. properly described on the proposal documents?

## 2. CONTENTS (INCLUDING CUPS, TROPHIES ETC.)

In the case of some clubs which are based in remote sites, it may not be possible to obtain contents insurance. Even if an underwriter is prepared to cover the risks, the premium may be so high as to be quite uneconomic.

Clubs with substantial silverware collections must make arrangements for insurance cover while trophies are out of the club premises. Few trophy winners will have sufficient personal or household insurance to cover a loss by destruction or theft, and most will expect (rightly or wrongly) that trophies will be covered by the club's own arrangements. In the case of old trophies in particular, replacement value may be very much more than the raw metal value; a regular revaluation is essential.

## 3. CASH
This is really an extension of the contents insurance section, with additional cover for cash in transit to and from the bank.

## 4. LOSS OF PROFITS
As in the case of any undertaking whose business could be affected by fire, flood or other damage to premises, or by burglary or malicious damage, a club which has to cancel an open meeting at short notice could find itself short of the budgeted income required to avoid a deficit. While it is inaccurate to speak of a members club making a "profit" or a "loss", this concept is easier for the insurance underwriter to grasp than "surplus" or "deficit" and accordingly insurance policies for clubs are phrased in those terms.

## 5. EMPLOYERS' LIABILITY
There is a statutory requirement for any employer to insure itself against liability for employees' accidental injury claims, and for the certificate of insurance to be exhibited prominently for inspection by all employees. In this context it is important that all employees, whether full time, part-time or seasonal, should be noted on the proposal form. An employee for this purpose is defined as a person who works for or on behalf of the club and under the direct or general supervision of the club. Thus for example a club which doubles as a training establishment and employs sailing coaches on a seasonal basis, at however modest a wage, will be obliged to insure against potential claims by such staff. If on the other hand volunteer trainers or coaches are appointed and given a general brief to conduct training courses, without any day-to-day supervision by the club, this will not amount to "employment".

Other staff, such as stewards, paid secretaries and bosuns come within the category of employees.

## 6. FIDELITY GUARANTEE

In the case of clubs employing staff to handle substantial cash transactions, a fidelity guarantee provides worthwhile protection when it is not possible for the management committee to exercise close supervision.

## 7. PUBLIC LIABILITY

In Chapter IV we examined the areas in which a club might become involved in third party claims. While it should be possible to structure club activities so as to reduce such liabilities to a minimum, insurance is essential against this most expensive potential form of loss. Recent awards in the English courts for personal injuries of over £500,000 indicate that a sum assured of £750,000 or £1m should now be sought as adequate protection.

In the case of clubs involved in training activities, public liability cover might be extended to protect coaches and instructors undertaking training on behalf of the club. A scheme has been devised by the RYA to provide a policy for qualified instructors taking full personal membership of the RYA to be covered for third party liability for death and personal injury, though not for property damage. Where members' vessels are used for training purposes, it will normally be more economical to invite the member to extend his own insurance policy to cover use for training, and for the club to undertake to meet any additional premium payable rather than for the club to extend its own policy to cover the vessel in question for a short period.

## 8. PERSONAL ACCIDENT

Members of an incorporated club, injured while involved in a club activity or on club business can rarely sue the club itself, since the club has no separate existence apart from its members.

The member would in effect be suing himself. A member may however sue a fellow member where the defendant by his own direct negligent act or omission has caused or contributed to an accident. It is for this eventuality that a personal accident "member-to-member extension" should be taken out, as no-one would wish to reduce a fellow member to penury as a result of his involvement in club activities.

## 9. PIERS, JETTIES AND PONTOONS

This is an extension to premises insurance but will normally be costed on a basis more appropriate to barges and floating vessels than to buildings, owing to the very much higher risk of accidental loss or damage suffered by such structures.

## 10. CLUB BOATS

The insurance arrangements applying to club boats will be subject to the terms and conditions of a standard marine policy. The following points should be noted:

### 10.1 Limitation of liability

It is a fundamental principle of marine insurance and liability that the owner of a vessel may limit his liability to escape the full financial consequences of his own or his employers' negligence. Before November 1986, the Merchant Shipping Acts provided that, in the case of property damage, the owner of a vessel could limit his liability to £40 per ton and, for personal injury or death, to a sum of £40,000 for craft under 300 tons. These archaic limits were raised in December 1986 to approximately £60,000 and £120,000 respectively, which will accordingly be the limit of the yacht club's liability, as owner, where club boats have caused or contributed to injury or damage.

### 10.2 Value of vessel

Marine insurance is unique in that the underwriters may not limit claims to "market value" as in the case of a car insurance, or to "replacement value" as in the case of a building. The marine insurance contract allows for an "agreed value" which will normally be the market value but which, for any number of good reasons, may by negotiation be considerably more (or less) than the market value. A false valuation stated by the insured on his proposal could be held by a court to be a "material non-disclosure" thus invalidating the policy in the event of a claim, unless the valuation is accompanied by some explanation as to why market value was inappropriate in that particular case.

### 10.3 Proposal form

As in all cases, the club must bear in mind that incorrect, inadequate or false information may entitle the underwriter to deny liability under the policy.

## 10.4  Periods of validity

In times past yachts and club boats were generally kept in commission for between five and eight months in each year. The modern practice is to extend this period. Many of the headings in the standard yacht or small craft policy do provide cover for a full twelve months but the club should stipulate the period in commission and the period laid-up. It is advisable, initially, to pay for no more months in commission than is necessary. If subsequently it is decided to extend the commission period, then the insurers should be informed and an additional premium agreed to cover the additional period.

## 10.5  Standard policy

Broadly speaking there are four main sections in the standard policy, all of which presuppose the craft is being used for pleasure purposes only. The cover includes:

(a) Loss of or damage to craft by marine perils up to the value insured. The cover includes sinking, stranding, fire, collision, theft of the vessel and, following forcible entry, theft of fittings and equipment belonging to the craft (defined as such items as would normally form part of the inventory of the craft upon sale).

(b) Collision with other craft resulting in damages for which the insured owner may be legally liable. This includes damage to piers, wharves and jetties etc. Removal of a wreck also comes within this section.

(c) Any legal liability for death, personal injury or property loss sustained by guests or other persons aboard (but excluding paid crew who should be insured seperately under the Employers' Liability Section).

(d) Salvage charges claimed by salvors. Reasonable charges for preventing losses are likely to be paid under most policies but this can be an area of doubt in some insurance contracts.

When completing proposal forms, bear in mind that motor craft with a design speed in excess of 17 knots are subject to special conditions (and higher premiums) and should be specifically referred to as such in the proposal form.

## 10.6  Territorial limits

There are three main standard ranges or areas, as follows:

(a) Full coastal and sea-going cruising within the home trade

46

limits which cover all United Kingdom waters and continental coasts from Brest to Elbe. Some policies may also include continental inland waters as far south as Paris.

(b) Coastal cruising within ten miles of home port or permanent moorings.

(c) Non-tidal waters of the United Kingdom.

All insurance policies will cover vessels while stored on land in the United Kingdom.

Any proposed cruise outside the cruising limits should be notified to underwriters. For example some insurers will require an additional premium to sail in Irish waters and the inland waterways of Europe.

### 10.7 Items covered

Although yacht and small craft insurance policies differ considerably, most will cover specifically the following items:

(a) The hull, rigging, sails, motor, tender "and other equipment" which includes a specified list which, in the case of cruising craft at least, includes one each of most of the obvious necessities.

(b) Trestles and tarpaulins but not trailers unless added by payment of an additional premium.

(c) Navigational risks and risks of launching.

(d) Fire risks. This is valid throughout the year and covers fire, explosion, lightning, aircraft or objects falling from an aircraft. Losses caused by action taken in anticipation or prevention of fire are also covered.

(e) Theft and wilful damage. This is also valid throughout the year and covers damage caused by unlawful taking of the boat and wilful damage caused by a person who is not a member of the club. If the theft or damage occurs other than within the area of a recognised boat club the insurance will only cover (except for theft of the entire boat) equipment belonging to the boat which is locked up, locked to the boat or otherwise fixed to the boat. Outboard motors must be attached to the boat by means of a lock. The words "forcible entry" are often important. Payment of a claim on most marine policies is only made "following forcible entry" and even then only on "gear, equipment or property specifically insured under the policy".

(f) Personal belongings. If a loss or damage can be classified under the headings above, underwriters will compensate for loss of members' personal belongings, but not in the event of the total loss of the boat unless a higher premium has been paid and the amount of the personal belongings declared. The general maximum compensation payable is £5000 (even if the total value of the goods is higher) and the maximum compensation for each object is £50. No compensation is paid for certain objects such as jewellery, money and objects of art. Personal belongings do not really form part of marine insurance and are often best covered under other sorts of policy, for example home contents.

## 10.8 Change of ownership
The policy is not normally transferable unless prior approval from the insurers has been given.

## 10.9 Exceptions
There is a considerable list of exceptions where underwriters will not compensate. These are, briefly, as follows:
(a) Where the boat is being used to earn money;
(b) If damage is caused deliberately, or through gross negligence;
(c) If the vessel is not properly equipped, or carelessly launched;
(d) Loss of an outboard motor dropped overboard;
(e) Damage caused by, or consisting of, faulty construction or materials, neglect or contamination;
(f) Loss of time or other indirect loss;
(g) Damage to buoys and moorings etc. These should be separately insured;
(h) No payment will be made unless the incident was the result of an external accidental cause. Thus, underwriters will not compensate for damage that would have happened in any event in the normal course of navigation, such as the splitting of seams on a very old, badly maintained vessel.

## 10.10 Chartering
As will be seen above, when a vessel is being used to earn money underwriters will not compensate. This point should be noted and special arrangements made in the case of club-

owned yachts available for use by members or where fellow members of a club enter into a charter agreement with an owner.

# VI

# LICENCES AND PUBLIC ACTS

## 1. LICENCES FOR THE SALE AND SUPPLY OF ALCOHOL

The members of a club who wish to be able to obtain intoxicating liquor on the premises may choose how they may do so lawfully.

The first approach is for the club to apply for a Justices' licence; the second is for the club to obtain a certificate of registration from the Magistrates' court. The distinction between Justices and Magistrates (who are usually the same individuals) for this purpose is that the Justices sit as a committee of between 5 and 15 persons, 5 to 9 times a year, to hear exclusively licensing business, whereas Magistrates will sit in fewer numbers on any day throughout the year, dealing with general business.

There are a number of practical distinctions between licensing and registration. If a club can show that it complies with the requirements of the Licensing Act 1964, the court is not entitled to refuse to grant a registration certificate. If an application is made for a Justices' licence, they have a discretion whether or not to grant a licence, and if a licence is granted, to attach conditions. While a licence needs to be renewed annually a club already registered for two years may have its registration certificate renewed for up to ten years. A licence will be subject to the normal licensing hours laid down by the Justices for the district, while a registered club may lay down its own hours for the supply of liquor.

The decision whether to apply for a licence or a registration certificate depends upon whether the liquor to be provided is the property of the members or of a separate proprietor. If the former, then the transaction will not be a sale, but a supply, in which case only a registration certificate will be required. The sale of alcohol on unlicensed premises is unlawful, whereas the supply to joint owners of alcohol is in principle unregulated, unless club premises are to be used in which case the Licensing Act requires a registration certificate to be obtained (or a licence as an alternative).

A club will be entitled to registration if it can comply with the following requirements under Section 41(2) of the Licensing Act.

(a) The club must be conducted in good faith as a club and have not less than twenty five members.

(b) The rules of the club must require an interval of at least two days between nomination or application for membership and admission to membership or to the privileges of membership.

(c) Alcoholic liquor must not be supplied to members on the premises otherwise than by or on behalf of the club.

(d) The purchase for the club and the supply by the club of intoxicating liquor must be managed by an elective committee. This is defined as a committee all of whom must be members of the club, elected in accordance with the provisions of Schedule 7(4) of the Act (reprinted in Appendix 4).

(e) No person may receive any commission or other special private benefit from the transaction at the expense of the club.

The question as to whether the club is "established and conducted in good faith as a club" permits the court to enquire into all the circumstances surrounding the running of the club, particularly with regard to any intention to sell alcoholic liquor to non-members. In the case of *The Little Ship Club* (1964) it was held that a provision in the rules to permit functions to be held for profit did not, of itself, destroy the applicants' claim that the club was run in good faith as a club; nor would a provision in the rules for visiting yachtsmen to purchase drinks destroy the bona fide element of the club. In *The Little Ship Club* case the High Court (hearing an appeal from the Magistrates) held that an alteration of the rules to permit the premises to be used for:

a) an unlimited number of functions to be held by other yacht clubs;

b) an unlimited number of functions to be held by club members for their private purposes; and

c) up to twelve functions a year for other unrelated functions;

at all of which non-members would buy drinks, did not destroy the good faith of the club.

It must be stressed that each certificate application and

renewal will be examined on its merits and the fact that one club is allowed certain concessions does not entitle another club necessarily to expect the same treatment.

The question of the qualification of an "elective committee" (defined in Schedule 7) depends, amongst other things, on all members having equal voting rights. In the case of the chairman or some other officer having a second, casting vote in elections this will disentitle the club from being absolved from the requirement to prove that it is established and managed in good faith as a club. In other words the Act makes this assumption in favour of a club whose rules comply exactly with the requirements of the Act. Clubs not complying are put to strict proof of their good faith.

## 1.1 Procedure for registration

Applications for registration must be in writing giving certain particulars about the applicant club. A standard form is given at Appendix 4. The form must specify the name, objects and address of the club, and shall state that the register of club members' names and addresses is kept at the club premises.

The application must also assert that each of the statutory requirements referred to above is satisfied. The names and addresses of the club officers, management committee and any relevant sub-committee shall also be given and, in the case of an application for a new certificate, a copy of the full club rules should accompany the application. If the application is for the renewal of a certificate, only the changes in the rules since the last hearing need be stated (or the full text of the rules may again be submitted if this is preferred).

The premises should be adequately described, together with a plan if the applicant believes this will facilitate the decision of the Magistrates.

The application should declare that the premises are, or will be, occupied by and habitually used for the purposes of the club. It should also state the times of opening and permitted hours, if any. Occupation in this context means that the club must be more than a mere licensee in premises occupied by some other person. Also to be declared is the nature of the club's occupation, whether freehold, leasehold or whatever, or whether none at all. If there is a landlord, his name and address should also be given and the address of other premises occupied by the club in the previous 12 months, together with detailed particulars of money borrowed by the club or charged against the club's property. Particulars should also be given of any liability, whether of the club or of a trustee, in respect of which any person has given a guarantee or provided security.

This information is required to establish that the club is conducted in good faith as a club from a financial as well as a constitutional aspect. Thus a loan from a brewery would be closely examined to ensure that despite the absence of a "tie" there was not some other underlying agreement regarding the purchase of liquor.

The application must be made (in triplicate) to the Clerk to the Justices of the area, (the two additional copies are sent to the Police Authority and the Local Authority). Public notice of the application must be given by display of a notice, or advertisement in a local newspaper.

## 1.2 Objections to the grant of a certificate

Objections to the grant or renewal of a certificate may be made by the Police, the Local Authority or any person affected as the occupier of other premises on the following grounds:

(a) That the club's application is incomplete or inaccurate or that some requirement of the Act has not been met;

(b) That the premises are not suitable and convenient because of their character and condition and the size and nature of the club;

(c) That the club is not qualified for registration;

(d) That the club is run in a disorderly way or that the rules for admission to membership are habitually disregarded;

(e) That the club is habitually used for an unlawful purpose, for indecent displays or as a resort of criminals or prostitutes;

(f) That there is frequent drunkenness or misconduct in the premises or misconduct relating to the supply of liquor.

The court must refuse an application if one of the above objections is proved. In addition to these grounds, the Police or Local Authority may also make representations as to conditions that should be imposed for the sale of liquor to non-members.

If the Magistrates refuse or cancel a certificate the club may appeal to the Crown Court and the Licensing Act provides that the club may be represented by the Chairman, Secretary, or any general committee member.

## 1.3  Permitted hours

The permitted hours of registered clubs should be established by the club rules but they should be no longer, nor begin earlier nor end later, than the general licensing hours. These are laid down in the Act as 11am to 10.30pm with a break of two and a half hours beginning at 3pm, or llam to 11pm, with the same break, if the Justices in the district have adopted the extended period provision in the Act. The Justices may alternatively have made a modification order under the Act allowing a total of nine or nine and a half hours, from 10am at the earliest to 10.30pm or llpm at the latest with a break of at least two hours in the afternoon.

On Christmas Day, Good Friday and Sundays the hours are from noon to 10.30pm with a break of five hours beginning at 2pm.

The above break times apply only to licensed premises. In the case of registered clubs, the rules must not only fix hours consistent with the local general licensing hours, but must also provide a break of at least two hours in the afternoon and, on Christmas Day, Good Friday and Sundays, a break from 3pm to 5pm and provide that there shall be no more than three and a half permitted hours after 5pm.

The Act provides, for licensed premises at least, that there is no requirement to be open for all permitted hours. It would be fair to assume that the same provision applies equally to registered clubs, although this is not spelt out in the Act.

## 1.4  Inspection

Where a club applies for a registration certificate the Local Authority, Fire Authority, and the Police all have the right to inspect the premises (on 48 hours notice) within 14 days of the date of applicaton.

## 1.5  Licensing

Some clubs may find it suits their requirements to hold a licence, even though qualified for registration, if for example they wish to be able to sell liquor to non-members. Applications for licences must give notice to the Clerk to the Justices, the Police and the Local Authority at least 21 days before a licensing session of the Justices and must advertise the proposed application for seven days on or near the premises in a prominent position and, between 14 and 28 days before the sessions, in a local newspaper. The notice to the Clerk must include a plan of the premises and the name, address and occupation of the applicant, who must be an officer of the club.

## 1.6 Special hours certificate

Licensees or registered clubs may apply to the Licensing Justices or Magistrates for a special hours certificate under the Licensing Acts 1976 — 1983. Seven days written notice of intention to apply must be given to the Justices and the Police. The hours available are from 12.30pm to 3pm and from 6.30pm to 2am (up to midnight if music and dancing is not provided).

## 1.7 Exemption order

Application may alternatively be made for a special order of exemption by which, at the discretion of the Justices or Magistrates, such hours as may be specified in the order are added to the permitted hours for special named occasions. "Special occasions" can extend over a period of days, such as regattas, boat shows etc. or can apply to a single event such as a dance or social meeting.

## 2. LOTTERIES AND RAFFLES

A lottery (and that term includes a raffle) is defined as "a scheme for the distribution of money by chance. It usually, if not always, takes the form of the creation of a fund by the participants in the lottery, who buy tickets or pay subscriptions in consideration of an offer by the promoters to award them a prize on some contingency the happening whereof depends on chance". Any genuine test of skill or judgement (such as listing the features of a boat in order of desirability or a "spot the buoy" competition) will not be a lottery and will not be subject to the Lotteries and Amusements Act 1976.

Under the terms of the 1976 Act all lotteries are unlawful except those for which special statutory provision is made. In the context of clubs, only small lotteries, private lotteries and societies' lotteries need be considered.

## 2.1  Small lotteries incidental to exempt entertainments

Section 3(2) of the 1976 Act defines "exempt entertainment" as a bazaar, sale of work, fête, dinner, dance, sporting or athletic event or any other event of a similar character whether taking place on one day or extending over two or more days. Whether an entertainment on the scale of the larger boat shows would fall within this category is unclear but the following conditions apply:

(a) Proceeds must not be for private gain;
(b) None of the prizes must be in money;
(c) All tickets must be sold on the premises during the entertainment;
(d) No more than £50 may be spent on prizes, although genuine gifts from sponsors may be of any value;
(e) There is no limitation on the price and number of tickets.

## 2.2  Private lotteries

A "private lottery" is a lottery promoted by members of a "society" established and conducted for purposes unconnected with gaming or lotteries.

The promoter of such a lottery must himself be a member of the group, authorised in writing by the governing body of the society. The conditions applying to such lotteries are that:

(a) The whole proceeds (less expenses for printing and stationery) must be devoted to the provision of prizes;
(b) The lottery may not be advertised except in the clubhouse.

Tickets must all be the same price and state the prize. Each ticket must bear on the face of it the name and address of the promoters and a statement of the persons to whom sale is restricted (i.e. members of the club or society) and a statement that no prize will be paid to any person other than the purchaser of the winning ticket.

## 2.3  Societies' lotteries

The main difference between societies' lotteries and the other two classes lies in the fact that tickets may be sold to the general public rather than confined to restricted groups of people. For this reason a very tight scheme of control is imposed by the 1976 Act.

"Society" in this context is defined as one formed for charitable, sporting or other non-commercial purpose. Bona fide sailing clubs clearly fall within this category. A lottery of this sort must comply with the following requirements:

(a) It must be promoted in Great Britain;

(b) The society must be registered with the Local Authority in which its headquarters (if any) is situated;

(c) The lottery must be promoted in accordance with a scheme approved by the society (in the case of most clubs the constitution is so framed as to include by inference authority for the management committee to give approval on behalf of the membership and it may be appropriate to minute an approval by the committee delegating this function to the secretary);

(d) If the total value of tickets or chances to be sold exceeds £5,000 the scheme must be registered with the Gaming Board for Great Britain.

(e) Once a society is registered and the "scheme" has been approved by the society the following requirements must be complied with:

— No more than 52 lotteries may be held in each year and a period of seven days must elapse between each one.

— Every promoter must be a member of the society and must be authorised in writing by the governing body.

— The maximum price of tickets is 50p.

— Every ticket must state the name of the society, the name and address of the promoter, the date of the lottery and the prize.

— Tickets not paid for in full may not be included in the draw and the return of money paid by participants is forbidden.

— Sale of tickets to or by a person under the age of 16 is prohibited.

— Tickets must not be sold in a street, in a betting shop, in amusement arcades, in gaming clubs, by vending machines, or at any person's home by a visitor discharging an official, professional or commercial function not connected with lotteries.

— Any advertisement must specify the name of the society, the name and address of the promoter and the date of the lottery.

— The proportion of the proceeds of a lottery appropriated for the provision of prizes must not be more than one half.

— If the total value of tickets is £5,000 or less, the

maximum value for prizes is £1,000.
— The whole proceeds of the lottery after prizes and expenses must be applied to the purposes of the society.
— Expenses incurred in relation to the lottery may be met out of proceeds provided they do not exceed more than 25% of the proceeds.

The promoter of a society's lottery must, not later than the end of the third month after the date of the lottery, send to the registration authority a return certified by two other members of the society.

The return must include a copy of the scheme under which the lottery was promoted and must show:
— The whole proceeds of the lottery;
— The sum appropriated for expenses;
— The sum appropriated for prizes;
— The purpose or purposes to which the proceeds were applied;
— The amount applied for each such purpose;
— The date of the lottery.

## 3. FRUIT MACHINES

Under the Gaming Act 1968, any club or similar establishment having gaming machines on its premises must obtain registration for the use of the machines from its local licensing authority. The Act also provides that no person may sell, supply or carry out maintenance on gaming machines unless he holds a valid certificate or permit issued by the Gaming Board. Any club which intends to install gaming machines on its premises or which already has them must ensure that the supplier or maintainer has a valid certificate.

## 4. PERFORMING RIGHTS SOCIETY

Under the terms of the Copyright Act 1956 it is unlawful to perform, whether live or by recording, or allow to be performed, any copyright music in public without the permission of the copyright owner. The term "in public" has been held to mean anywhere outside the domestic circle so that even background music played in a sailing club bar is public, whether or not entry is limited to club members.

The Performing Rights Society is an association of composers, authors and publishers of musical works established to administer the collection of royalty payments on behalf of its 17,000 members, controlling the public performance rights in most of the copyright music played in the United Kingdom. A PRS licence is necessary for practically every public performance of copyright music.

The PRS will normally grant a licence to any prospective music user, provided only that the person concerned is prepared to enter into a standard form of licence contract and pay a standard royalty.

Licences issued by the PRS are in the form of annual contracts which run from year to year until cancelled by either party. These are blanket licences which authorise the public performance of any of the millions of works which the PRS controls on behalf of its members and affiliated societies throughout the world. Royalties payable vary from time to time as the nature or extent of music usage changes in the premises concerned. Licences cover both live performances and performances by "mechanical" means, such as radios, tape and record players. They are issued for numerous categories of premises, sporting and social clubs falling within "tariff J". This tariff is divided into a number of components, distinguishing between featured live music, featured recorded music (i.e. music played at a specific function) and background music. At 1986 prices, a fee of £1.26 per function up to a maximum of £63.00 is levied and, for background music, an annual fee of £26.25 for a radio set and £57.75 for a record or tape player. PRS inspectors have been known to suggest substantial fees without investigating the use to which equipment is put. In one case a fee of £230.00 was reduced to £30.00 by negotiation, so it is well worth taking a critical look at your PRS licence fee, where appropriate.

Where a club occasionally opens its doors to persons other than members and guests (i.e. it holds some sort of public function) then it will find that it is required to pay an additional fee to the PRS based on the number of such events and the capacity of the function room.

Further sections of the licence cover TVs, videos and juke boxes which are levied at a set of scale rates.

## 5.  DATA PROTECTION ACT 1984

The Data Protection Register was established in November 1985. Following the six month introductory period, it is now an offence for certain computer users (data users) to hold personal data (i.e. any information about a living individual) unless registered as a data user.

## 5.1 Principles

The Act was introduced to comply with our obligation under the Council of Europe Convention for the Protection of Individuals with regard to Automatic Processing of Personal Data, which itself introduces eight fundamental principles:

(a) The information to be contained in personal data shall be obtained, and personal data shall be processed, fairly and lawfully.

(b) Personal data shall be held only for specified and lawful purposes.

(c) Personal data held for any purpose shall not be used or disclosed in any manner incompatible with that purpose.

(d) Personal data held for any purpose shall be adequate, relevant and not excessive in relation to that purpose.

(e) Personal data shall be accurate and, where necessary, kept up to date.

(f) Personal data held for any purpose shall not be kept for longer than is necessary for that purpose.

(g) An individual shall be entitled:
   (i) at reasonable intervals and without undue delay and expense:
   — to be informed by any data user whether he holds personal data of which that user is the subject; and
   — to have access to any such data held by a data user; and
   (ii) where appropriate, to have such data corrected or erased.

(h) Appropriate security arrangements shall be taken against unauthorised access to, or alteration, disclosure or destruction of, personal data and against accidental loss or destruction of personal data.

These principles should be followed by all data users. These are persons who control the contents and use of data.

"Data" is defined as "information recorded in a form in which it can be processed by equipment operating automatically in response to instructions given for that purpose".

Data is personal data if it consists of "information which

relates to a living individual who can be identified from the information". That does not necessarily involve holding a name on the record; an address or description can suffice.

There is no direct obligation on data users under the Act to comply with the data protection principles; these are enforced indirectly through the Registrar who has wide powers to direct, restrict and ultimately to de-register data users who fail to comply with the data protection principles.

## 5.2 Enforcement

If the Registrar is satisfied that a registered person has contravened any of the data protection principles, he may serve an enforcement notice requiring certain steps to be taken. The Registrar is required to consider whether the contravention has caused or is likely to cause distress or damage. The user may be required:

(a) to rectify or erase data; or
(b) to record the fact that the data in question has been obtained from a third party and that the data subject has objected to the data, and to include a statement of the true facts.

## 5.3 Appeals

An appeal may be made to the Data Protection Tribunal against:

(a) a refusal by the Registrar to register or to accept an alteration of registered particulars; or
(b) any of the Registrar's notices.

## 5.4 Registration

The entry on the register (application for which should be made to the Data Protection Registrar, Springfield House, Water Lane, Wilmslow, Cheshire SK9 5AX) must contain the following details:

(a) Name and address of the data user and company number if appropriate;
(b) A description of the data and the purposes for which it is used;
(c) A description of the sources of the data (for example, competitors in club events, club members);
(d) A description of the recipients of the data (for example, club officers);
(e) Other countries where data may be sent;

(f) Address to which data subjects should apply for access to their records.

Data must only be used in accordance with the registration details. It is therefore important to notify the Registrar of any changes of use etc.

## 5.5 Exemptions

So far as RYA affiliated clubs are concerned, personal data held by incorporated clubs cannot be exempt, but data held by unincorporated members' clubs is exempt on condition that the data subjects are all members of the club who have been asked if they object to the data being held and have not objected. In practice this can be achieved in the first instance by posting a notice on the club notice board stating that information within the scope of the Data Protection Act is held on computer by the Secretary/Treasurer and that any member of the club objecting to such data being held should contact the Secretary/Treasurer. Thereafter, at the time of the next Annual General Meeting, the members should be invited to approve an addition to the club rules as follows:

"Membership of the club and acceptance of these rules by the member will be deemed to constitute consent to the holding of relevant personal data for the purposes of the Data Protection Act 1984".

Unincorporated members' clubs keeping open meeting records or other records involving non-members are not entitled to this exemption and must therefore either register themselves, or, if affiliated to the RYA, join the RYA block registration.

In summary the significance of the Act for clubs is as follows:

(a) Any club not coming within the exemption mentioned above, and using computerised records, is required to register;

(b) Individuals whose data are recorded with a non-exempt club will be able to require that the club to disclose on request any data stored by that body;

(c) If the data stored is inaccurate, or should the club disclose information without an individual's consent, it could find itself liable for damages;

(d) The Registrar has power to de-register any organisation. If a non-exempt club finds itself the subject of a number of complaints by members due to its disclosing information illegally or storing incorrect information, it may find itself having to cease using its computer or wordprocessor for the relevant purpose.

(e) The club may find itself the subject of enquiries from individuals asking for full details of what is recorded and this may cause an administrative burden.

While it is clear that the Registrar has considerable powers of entry, search and prosecution, it is not likely that substantial penalties will be imposed for purely technical offences — where for instance a registration form has been incorrectly completed but no damage has resulted or would be likely to result.

## 6. HEALTH AND SAFETY AT WORK ACT 1974

Section 2(3) of the Act provides that every employer (except where exempted, as in the case of employers employing less than 5 employees) shall prepare, and as often as may be appropriate revise, a written statement of his general policy with respect to the health and safety at work of his employees and the organization and arrangements in force for carrying out that policy, and bring the statement and revisions to the notice of all his employees. Failure to comply with this requirement is a criminal offence.

As will be seen at Appendix 7, the required statement need not be a complex documment so long as the following aspects are covered:

(a) The general policy statement should be a declaration of the employer's intent to seek to provide the safest and healthiest working conditions possible and to enlist the support of his employees in achieving these ends.

(b) The statement should identify the person responsible for fulfilling the policy.

(c) All individuals at every level will have to accept degrees of responsibility for carrying out that policy. Where appropriate, key individuals should be named and their responsibilities defined.

(d) The policy statement should make it clear that the final level of responsibility is that of each individual.

(e) The written statement should ensure that all who are at risk are well aware of the hazards, the reasons for control in working practices and the part that they as individuals have to play in ensuring a safe and healthy working environment.

(f) Potential danger areas should be identified and procedures laid down for accidents, particularly those involving personal injury, to be systematically recorded by an employee. Any information, based on expert analyses of accidents or dangerous occurences, should be monitored by the employer and brought to the attention of the relevant employees.

Secretaries and principals wishing to obtain more information about their responsibilities under the Act should contact the Health and Safety Executive, Baynards House, 1 Chepstow Place, London W2 4TF (01 229 3456).

## 7.  FIRE REGULATIONS

### 7.1   A club licensed or registered to sell alcohol

The Licensing Justices have an absolute discretion to refuse the renewal of a licence, under the Licensing Act 1964, or to make such conditions as they consider to be in the public interest, including the making of an order for structional alterations to the premises. Their discretion must be exercised judicially and not in an arbitrary manner but the Justices are not limited as to the kinds of objection that they may take into consideration. An appeal lies to the Crown Court against the attachment of conditions to a licence but the conditions would have to be clearly unreasonable to give rise to any likelihood of a successful appeal.

### 7.2   All clubs

Under the Fire Precautions Act 1971, any premises used for the purposes of entertainment, recreation or instruction or for the purposes of any club, society or association must obtain a fire certificate issued by the Fire Authority. A certificate may only be issued where fire fighting precautions have been taken and means of escape provided. If the Fire Authority is not satisfied, it must notify the applicant of the steps necessary to satisfy the requirements and specify a time within which those steps are to be taken.

A fire certificate, when issued, may impose such requirements as the fire authority considers appropriate in the circumstances.

Any person aggrieved by the conditions of issue of a certificate may appeal within 21 days to the court which may make such order as it thinks fit.

## 8. OFFICES, SHOPS AND RAILWAY PREMISES ACT 1963

This Act applies to all such premises where people (even one solitary person) are employed. The definition of office premises includes any room used for administrative or clerical work, even if only forming a small part of a club, but not a club room or bar where entry is restricted to members only and one corner is occasionally used for clerical work by an employee.

The purpose of the Act is to ensure safe and hygenic working conditions for employees. A summary of the main provisions is given below. Any person intending to employ people in an office must notify the local authority who will provide an application form for the registration of the premises. In summary the Act provides as follows:

**Section 4** Cleanliness — All premises, furniture, furnishings and fittings must be kept in a clean state. No dirt or refuse must be allowed to accumulate, and floors and steps must be cleaned at least once a week by washing or sweeping.

**Section 5** Overcrowding — A room in which people work must not be so overcrowded as to cause risk of injury to health. For this purpose regard must be paid not only to the number of people in the room but also to the amount of space occupied by furniture, fittings, machinery etc. A room where people work must provide at least 40 square feet of floor space for each normal occupant, or 400 cubic feet where the ceiling is lower than 10ft.

**Section 6** Temperature — A reasonable temperature must be maintained in every relevant room. This is defined as not less than 16°C (60.8°F) after the first hour. Means of heating likely to cause injurious or offensive fumes are prohibited. A thermometer must be conspicuously placed for the benefit of employees.

**Section 7** Ventilation — There must be effective and suitable means of ventilation by the circulation of adequate supplies of fresh air.

**Section 8** Light — Suitable and sufficient natural or artificial light must be provided in every part of the premises where people work or pass. Windows and skylights must be kept clean and free from obstruction so far as reasonably practicable but they can be whitewashed or shaded to mitigate heat or glare. Artificial lighting apparatus must be properly maintained.

**Sections 9 & 10** Sanitary conveniences & washing facilities — Suitable and sufficient sanitary conveniences must be provided in accordance with the Sanitary Convenience and Washing Facility Regulations. These provide that adequate facilities should be provided (separate male and female if 6 or more persons, regardless of sex, are employed), with a space with means of ventilation between WC and any workroom, under cover, with suitable privacy and screening. Fixed handbasins with a supply of hot and cold or warm water and a waste pipe with the same requirement for separate male/female accomodation as for WCs under cover with effective ventilation.

**Section 11** Drinking water — An adequate supply of wholesome water must be provided, either piped or replenished daily, with drinking vessels also provided, either disposable or with rinsing facilities, unless drinking water is available from a jet.

**Section 12** Clothing — Arrangements must be made for clothing not worn during working hours to be hung up and aired.

**Section 14** Seats for sedentary workers must be suitable in design, construction and dimensions for the worker and for the kind of work done. A foot rest must be provided unless it is possible to support the feet comfortably without one. Both the seat and the footrest must be properly supported while in use.

**Section 16** Floors, passages and stairs must be soundly constructed and properly maintained and so far as possible kept free from obstruction and slippery substances. Staircases must have a proper handrail, on the open side if there is one or on both sides if both are open.

**Section 24** First aid — A first aid box containing only first aid requisites must be provided for the use of employees and must be readily accessible. The contents must comply with the statutory regulations available from the Local Authority.

**Sections 28, 33 & 38** Means of escape from fire — must be available at all times, workrooms must be so laid out as not to prevent escape from fire, and adequate fire fighting equipment must be provided (which in the case of small premises may necessitate no more than buckets of water or hand held extinguishers).

**Section 29** — Only occupiers of premises where more than 20 people are employed, or more than 10 other than on the ground floor, need apply for a fire certificate from the local fire authority.

## 9. FIREARMS REGULATIONS

A "firearm", properly so called, is "any lethal barrelled weapon of any description from which any shot, bullet or other missile can be discharged".

A "shotgun" is "a smooth bore gun having a barrel not less than twenty four inches in length".

It is an offence to buy or have in one's possession a firearm or a shotgun (or ammunition for either) without the appropriate certificate. Firearms and shotgun certificates are obtained by applying to the Chief Officer of Police for the area in which the applicant resides. Certificates have a validity of three years and a fee is ordinarily payable. No fee should be payable if the Chief Officer of Police can be satisfied that a firearm or ammunition is required as part of the equipment of a ship.

There are two exceptions to the requirement for having a certificate:

(a) A person may have in his possession a firearm or ammunition on board a ship as part of the equipment of the ship. This exception also applies to shotguns although it is difficult to see how a shotgun could legitamately form part of the equipment of a ship.

(b) A person may carry a firearm or shotgun (or ammunition for either) belonging to another person if the former has a certificate under instructions from and for the use of that other person for sporting purposes only.

### 9.1 Starting guns

The ordinary starting cannon used by many yacht clubs is undoubtedly a 'firearm' and a certificate should be held by the club using it, or the club secretary. The person actually firing the cannon should be under the club's or the club secretary's instructions and it is probably best that written instructions are given; these could be in general terms and brought to the attention of the race officer concerned.

### 9.2 Distress signals

A Very pistol is clearly a 'firearm' as is a 'Dial-a-Star'. If carried on board as part of the equipment of the yacht, no firearm certificate is required. If the pistol is taken ashore for storage, although a certificate is not required, a permit must be obtained from the police covering its removal, storage and replacement on board. It is probably less bother to apply for a certificate for a Very pistol, which will be issued free and will last for three years, if the pistol is to be part of the equipment of the yacht.

Many yachtsmen may have in their possession "Miniflares" made by Schermuly. The Police have in the past treated these as 'firearms'. The manufacturers have however completely redesigned the launching mechanism so that equipment now sold can no longer be described as a firearm and accordingly no licence is necessary on the current version.

## 10. VHF

### 10.1 Ashore

A yacht club wishing to operate a base station, on Channel M or other private channels, will require a Private Mobile Radio Licence. Applications should be made to the Department of Trade and Industry, Radio Communications Division, Waterloo Bridge House, Waterloo Road, London SE1 8UA, tel: 01 275 3000. Licences may be granted for a base station and up to nine mobile stations on Channel M. Shore-based use of Channel M does not require a qualified operator as this frequency is not in the International Maritime VHF Band. However, regular users should be encouraged to obtain the Certificate of Competence in Radiotelephony, restricted VHF only.

### 10.2 Afloat

With the exception of the mobile stations operated under a yacht club's base station licence, every maritime VHF radio must have its own licence. Two types of licence are available:

Ship Radio Licence (VHF);

Ship Radio (Transportable) Licence.

The first of these is the usual form of licence for the use of a maritime VHF radio on board a particular vessel. The Transportable Licence allows the radio to be used on any number of different vessels using the name of that vessel for identification. With a Transportable Licence, you are limited in the channels you may use. For example, no Public Correspondence channels may be used and therefore no link calls may be made. As no particular vessel is licensed for radio equipment, no call sign is allocated.

Equipment, whether shore-based or aboard ship, must meet certain minimum type-approval standards.

VHF equipment in every vessel shall be under the control of an operator holding at least the Certificate of Competence in Radiotelephony, restricted VHF only. An Authority to Operate is also required to operate a ship radio station on board a vessel which is entitled to fly the British flag. The Authority to Operate may be issued at the same time as the Certificate of Competence. Application forms for the examination for the Certificate of Competence in Radiotelephony, restricted VHF only, can be obtained from RYA Head Office.

# VII

# CLUB LEASES

## 1. DISTINCTION BETWEEN LEASE AND LICENCE

Unless a club is in the fortunate position of owning its own freehold site and having free access to sailing water, it will normally occupy its premises as lessee or licensee.

It is important to know whether the agreement in force is a lease or a licence, as this has a direct bearing on the level of protection afforded by the law and in particular the Landlord and Tenant Act 1954. Whether an agreement gives rise to a tenancy depends on the exact terms, irrespective of the title given to it by the parties.

A lease is defined as the grant of the exclusive possession of land for a determinate period. A licence on the other hand is a mere personal privilege, a permission that negates trespass. All lessees (tenants) necessarily have exclusive possession. Some licences give exclusive possession, some do not.

Where the agreement is in documentary form, whatever label may have been given to it by the parties, if it in fact confers on the parties the rights and obligations normally associated with a landlord and a tenant, then it will be a lease.

To take two examples: the granting of "the right to train and exercise racehorses on the gallops" under which the tenant enjoyed complete control of the area was held to amount to a tenancy.

Where on the other hand a canal company granted the "sole and exclusive liberty" of putting pleasure boats for hire on the canal, this was merely a licence, since the canal remained open for other purposes to other persons.

### 1.1 Covenants: express and implied

The conditions and mutual promises entered into by parties to a lease are binding on each party. Where covenants to repair, or to use the premises for a specified purpose, or not to sublet, are expressly stated in the lease, this needs no explanation.

There are however a number of conditions that impliedly

attach to every lease, even if not stated in the agreement.

Perhaps the most important of these is the landlord's implied covenant to give the tenant quiet enjoyment of the premises. By a covenant for quiet enjoyment the tenant is entitled to enjoy his lease without interruption from the landlord or his representative, even if such interruption would otherwise be lawful.

Similarly, every landlord impliedly covenants not to 'derogate from the grant' when he retains land adjacent to that comprised in the tenancy. This applies in most inland sailing club and school leases where the water authority or other landlord lets off a small part of its land or water to a club or school.

In practice the covenant against derogation means that the landlord may not use his own (i.e. unlet, or let to another party) land so as to render the tenant's holding less suitable for the purpose for which it is let.

Thus if a local authority were to plant a substantial belt of trees immediately adjacent to a reservoir or lake which it had let for sailing purposes, that could amount to a derogation, as could the blocking-up of access or lowering of water levels for other purposes (although in some leases the right to reduce the water level is expressly reserved).

## 1.2  Rent reviews

Most leases now incorporate rent review clauses which allow for increases every three or five years. The RYA carries out periodic surveys of inland water rents throughout the country and the figures abstracted from these surveys have often proved helpful to clubs negotiating a review.

Because it is more difficult to "price" a reservoir or gravel pit than a shop or office building, it is essential that a club facing what it believes to be an unreasonable rent review should enlist the services of a qualified surveyor on a professional basis. The RYA is able to provide a list of surveyors experienced in this field who have previously acted successfully for RYA affilliated clubs. Not only do these surveyors have the experience and ability to achieve the best rent for a club, human nature also dictates that the landlord's surveyor will be more amenable to negotiation with one of his own kind.

While a negotiated settlement of a rent review is always to be preferred, it is important that the club should be aware of the criteria governing the fixing of rents, and how those criteria differ from the pricing of commercial leases. For example it is now accepted that in the case of a voluntary members' club with a covenant limiting the premises to use as a sailing club, the square footage of the club premises is of secondary relevance only, the determining factor being the ability of the club to attract members in sufficient numbers and at sufficient subscription, to enable the club to operate without the rent bill causing a deficit to be run up.

## 2. TERMINATION AND RENEWAL OF TENANCIES

### 2.1 Landlord and Tenant Act 1954

Section 23 of the Act provides that a tenancy qualifies under Part II of the Act if property is occupied by the tenant for the purposes of a business carried on by him. Personal occupation is not essential, nor the carrying on of a business in the property, provided that the property or some part of it is occupied for the purposes of a business carried on by the tenant.

The word "business" includes any activity carried on by a body of persons, whether corporate or unincorporate. The leading case of *Addiscombe Garden Estates v. Crabbe* (1958) arose from the occupation of premises by an unincorporated members' tennis club. The principle established in that case holds good for all members' clubs and applies as much to dinghy parks and gravel pits or reservoirs as to tennis courts.

This principle presupposes that the club uses the premises for its purposes with the knowledge and consent of the landlord.

In contrast to the Rent Acts (which afford protection for private residential lettings) it is not a condition of the 1954 Act that a rent should be payable under the tenancy. When a new tenancy by order of the court is granted, the tenant must however expect to pay a rent.

A number of tenancies are excluded from the operation of the Act. The only categories relevant for our purposes are:-
(a) Tenancies for a fixed term of less than six months without a renewal provision where neither the tenant nor his predecessor occupied the premises before the start of the tenancy; and
(b) Tenancies contractually excluded where the court (normally the relevant local County Court) has

authorised an agreement between the parties that the protection provisions of the Act should not apply.

Tenancies to which Part II of the Act applies, whether fixed term or periodic, are by Section 24(1) continued automatically after the agreed term has expired, until brought to an end by a special form of statutory notice given by the landlord or the tenant, or until the occurrence of certain other contingencies.

The landlord is empowered by Section 25 to terminate the tenancy by a notice given in a specified form. The tenant is empowered by Section 26 to terminate the current tenancy by making a request for a new tenancy in accordance with the provisions of that section. Termination under either of these sections entitles the tenant, by taking the appropriate steps, to apply for a new tenancy under the Act.

The current tenancy can also come to an end in certain other ways so that a continuation tenancy does not arise. Thus a notice to quit given by the tenant or a surrender of the lease or forfeiture for breach of covenant will conclusively terminate the tenancy.

As we have seen, when the contractual tenancy comes to an end, it is not essential that a new tenancy under the Act should immediately take its place. The new tenancy comes into existence either by an order of the court under Section 29, or by an agreement between the parties under Section 28. In the meantime Section 24(1) provides for the old tenancy simply to carry on automatically without any action required by either party. All terms and conditions of the old tenancy (except any provisions for termination) will continue to govern the continuation tenancy.

It often happens that the parties have the right in the lease to terminate the agreement giving a period of notice, typically six months. The effect of the Act is that, even if the landlord does give such a notice, this serves only to terminate the agreement; the tenancy (i.e. the right to occupy) continues until terminated in accordance with the strict provisions of the Act. However, a Section 25 notice correctly served in accordance with the Act can terminate both the contract and the tenancy.

## 2.2 Landlord's notice to terminate a tenancy

A landlord wishing to terminate must do so in the prescribed form to take effect between six and twelve months after service of the notice. The notice must require the tenant, within two months of the date of the notice, to inform the landlord in writing whether or not at the date of termination the tenant will be prepared to give up possession.

The notice must also indicate whether the landlord would oppose an application under the Act for the grant of a new tenancy and, if so, on which of the grounds in Section 30 he would do so.

No statutory form of counter-notice is prescribed by the Act. An informal notice which makes plain the tenant's intentions is sufficient, although it may be wise to use the form of wording as follows:-

"To                , of                , the landlord of premises known as
1.  I,                          of                          ,
    the secretary [or trustee] of the above-named club acknowledge receipt of your notice dated the [   ] day of [     ] to terminate the tenancy of the premises and hereby give you notice that we are not willing to give up possession of the premises on the date specified in your said notice.
2.  This notice is given under the provisions of Section 25(5) of the Landlord and Tenant Act 1954.
Dated                          Signed                          ”

For the tenant who wishes to retain possession it is equally important that the counter-notice is served within the two months allowed.

### 2.3  Tenant's application for a new tenancy

As an alternative to awaiting the landlord's notice and serving a counter-notice, tenants who are unwilling to carry on in occupation under the terms of the continuation tenancy may themselves serve a notice under Section 26 requesting a new tenancy. Here again the request must be made in the form prescribed by the Act, setting out the tenant's proposals as to the property to be comprised in the new tenancy, the date from which the tenancy is to commence (being between six and twelve months from the date of notice and not earlier than the expiry of the previous contractual tenancy), the length of tenancy asked for, the rent to be payable and the other terms of the new tenancy.

For his part the landlord is entitled within two months of the notice to give notice to the tenant that he will oppose the application stating the grounds of his opposition.

The tenant must, whether or not the landlord has served a counter-notice, apply to the court for a new tenancy between two and four months after the making of the request.

If the tenant fails to make this application, the current tenancy ends immediately before the date specified by the tenant in his request for a new tenancy and he loses all his rights under the Act.

Where, after the tenant has applied to the court for a new tenancy, the parties reach agreement on all the terms of a proposed new tenancy, the tenant may withdraw his application.

## 2.4 Grounds of opposition available to landlord

The landlord's grounds for opposing a new tenancy are set out in Section 30(1) of the Act. He may however, when in court, only rely on such grounds as he has specified in his notice or counter-notice to the tenant.

### 2.4.1 *Breach of repairing obligation*

Mere proof that the tenant has been in breach does not of itself entitle the landlord to have the tenant's application dismissed. The breach has to be such that the tenant "ought not" be granted a new tenancy. Thus the court has a discretion to consider the seriousness of the breach in relation to the state of repair of the holding generally. The court may take into account an offer by the tenant that the new tenancy should contain a convenant obliging him forthwith to put the premises into repair in accordance with the repairing covenants in the previous lease.

### 2.4.2 *Persistent delay in paying rent*

Here again the court has a discretion in assessing the seriousness of the delay. "Persistent delay" implies a course of conduct over a period of time. The court will take into account all the circumstances of the case and whether the landlord can be adequately safeguarded for the future, for instance by being granted security for prompt payment.

### 2.4.3 *Breaches of other obligations*

It will be a question of fact for the court to decide whether breaches are such that the tenant "ought" to be deprived of a new tenancy. Any kind of waiver of, or acquiescence in, a breach by the landlord will clearly militate strongly against the refusal of a new tenancy on the grounds of the breach. The court is entitled to look at all the circumstances in connection with the breach and the general conduct of the tenant in the past.

### 2.4.4 Availability of alternative accommodation

If the landlord has offered suitable alternative accommodation for the tenant and the terms of his offer are reasonable having regard to the terms of the current tenancy, then the court has no discretion to order a new tenancy. If suitable alternative accommodation is offered, then the tenant may have to make a fast decision since the landlord does not have to hold the offer open for any specified length of time and the tenant's failure to accept an offer will virtually guarantee the failure of his application for a new tenancy.

### 2.4.5 Possession required for letting or otherwise disposing of the property as a whole

A new tenancy may be successfully opposed by the landlord where the tenancy was formed by subletting part of a superior tenancy and the superior landlord is able to let the whole property for more than the parts. To succeed on this ground the landlord must be able to show that the superior tenancy will have come to an end by the date on which the applicant's current tenancy is due to terminate.

### 2.4.6 Landlord's intention to demolish or reconstruct

The tenancy may also be validly terminated where on the termination of the tenancy the landlord intends to demolish or reconstruct the premises comprised in the holding or a substantial part of those premises, or to carry out a substantial work of reconstruction which he could not reasonably perform without obtaining possession of the holding. The intention of the landlord must be genuine, firm and settled and not likely to be changed. The court will more easily be satisfied of the landlord's intention if the premises are old and worn out and ripe for redevelopment.

### 2.4.7 Landord's intention to occupy holding

This will apply where, on the termination of the tenancy, the landlord intends to occupy the premises for the purposes of his business, or as his residence. This ground can only be relied on by the landlord if he has been the owner of the premises for at least 5 years before the termination of the current tenancy.

## 2.5 Order for new tenancy

Where the court finds in favour of the tenant, a new tenancy must be ordered on terms, at a rent, and for a duration, to be decided upon after hearing evidence from both parties (normally expert evidence of surveyors) as to what is reasonable and having regard to the terms of the original tenancy. The maximum length of new tenancy is 14 years. The rent to be ordered is that at which the premises might reasonably be expected to be let on the open market (see also paragraph 1.2 above).

## 2.6 Compensation

The Act provides for the tenant to be compensated where the court is precluded under paragraphs 2.4.5-7 above from granting a new tenancy.

The amount of compensation will be six times the rateable value of the premises where the premises have been occupied for the purposes of the tenant's business for 14 years or more; if less it will be three times the rateable value.

Provision is also made in the Act for the outgoing tenant to be compensated for improvements where the landlord has been informed of, and did not object to, the improvements before they were carried out. The sum awarded may not exceed the net addition to the value of the holding. Compensation may be deferred, and indeed not paid at all, if the landlord intends to redevelop the property so as to negate the effects of the improvements.

## 3. DEALINGS WITH LANDLORDS

### 3.1 Crown Estate Commissioners

Under the terms of the Crown Estates Act 1961, the Commissioners are charged with the function of managing the Crown Estate and turning the Estate to account, which can be interpreted as a requirement to raise the highest possible rent from their assets.

Since the Crown Estate comprises virtually all the fundus in Great Britain, from the high water mark to the limit of territorial jurisdiction, it is clear that the major source of income from this part of the estate consists of rents and licence fees paid by harbour authorities, marina and mooring authorities, and clubs and private individuals paying for the right to lay moorings.

As rent can be demanded by any landowner as a condition of granting a lease or licence, so the Commissioners are entitled to levy a fee for the right to use the fundus, or seabed, for mooring purposes.

Since the monopoly position of the Commissioners could, in theory, be abused so as to hold the country to ransom, a number of quasi-statutory and customary provisions apply so as to ensure that, so far as possible, the rents levied by the Commissioners are fair and reasonable.

### 3.1.1 *The role of the District Valuer*

In the course of the parliamentary debate on the 1961 Act, the Minister agreed that in cases of dispute the Commissioners should submit the issue to the District Valuer, an official usually appointed by the Inland Revenue, to whom both parties should feel confident to look to for a fair arbitration. The Commissioners almost invariably adopt the practice of submitting all rent reviews to the DV without waiting for a dispute to arise. In most cases this works fairly; the DV understands his position as "arbitrator" and is ready to hear reasoned arguments as to the level of rent to be charged for a holding, be it a block of moorings, a pontoon or a slipway. In some areas however it is clear that the DV misunderstands the background to his appointment and appears to act as the agent of the Commissioners in attempting to wrest the highest possible rent from the lessee concerned. Where there is evidence that the DV is misdirecting himself as to his status, the tenant should ask to see the terms of reference under which he was appointed.

### 3.1.2 *Conditions affecting the Commissioners*

Section 3(1) of the Crown Estate Act 1961 provides that "the Commissioners shall not sell, lease or otherwise dispose of any land of the Crown Estate, or any right of privilege over or in relation to any such land, except for the best consideration in money or money's worth which in their opinion can be reasonably obtained, having regard to all the circumstances of the case but excluding any element of monopoly value attributable to the extent of the Crown's ownership of comparable land".

Interpreted literally this would mean that the Commissioners should always attempt to secure the best market price for land subject only to the fiction that a private adjacent landlord is competing for the lease. Clearly this would lead to inordinately high rents and accordingly two non-statutory conventions or practices have been adopted.

### 3.1.3  *Facility for public use*
Where a facility is for the use of the public, such as a playing field or a mooring area taken by a club, rent will be charged on the basis of this being for the public benefit rather than for commercial benefit. This results in reasonable rents being charged and in practice at 1987 levels a bracket of £20-£30 pa per individual mooring site can be expected, and of £30-£150 for slipways, in each case depending on the site, condition, demand etc. of the facility.

### 3.1.4  *Restriction on "mark-up"*
Where a mooring area is let to a club or a harbour authority, the lessee is permitted to sublet individual sites to boatowners and to add an amount to that portion of the rent attributable to each site to cover administration costs and build up a reserve to cover any future deficit. This "mark-up" is subject to a 25% limit which is intended to prevent clubs or authorities making a profit from what is, after all, a public facility, in public ownership.

### 3.2  **Water Authorities**
There are estimated to be over 150 inland water sailing clubs using Water Authority facilities, for the most part compensation or water supply reservoirs. Until the 1970s it was rare to see any water authority reservoir put to public use, but the new duty, under Section 20 of the 1973 Water Act, to "make facilities available for sport and recreation so far as reasonably practicable," resulted in the rapid growth in available facilities in the early 1970s. At that time many clubs were established to cope with the dinghy sailing boom, often on peppercorn or at most heavily discounted rents, as it was clear that the parties had little idea what sort of fee could reasonably be charged for a facility.

For the most part the Water Authorities have proved to be good landlords. A well managed and popular facility provides an attractive public showpiece for what is otherwise

79

a low-profile organisation, and for some years rents were maintained at reasonable levels. There is now however increasing pressure on all public authorities to make their books balance, and each individual activity is subject to closer scrutiny for profitability. It is not within the scope of this book to examine Water Authority accounting practices, but clubs facing typical 5-yearly rent renewals in 1986/87 are often asked for a figure 3 times the existing rent against an RPI rise of some 40% over that 5-year period. The prospect of privatisation of Water Authorities is unlikely to reduce this pressure.

When faced with an unacceptatble increase (and research shows that figures equivalent to £15 and £25 per boat in dinghy parks for landlord-built and self-built facilities respectively are the top end of what is reasonable to pay in normal circumstances) it is essential to obtain early professional advice. This is so for two reasons: Firstly, only a surveyor experienced in reservoir valuations can give a real indication of what the facilities are worth. He will have experience of other negotiations and his experience will invariably justify his fee many times over. Secondly, professional surveyors acting for the landlord will always prefer to negotiate with one of their own kind rather than a gifted amateur, regrettable though such an attitude might be.

In the mid-1980s there is evidence of a decline in the popularity of dinghy sailing on inland waters. Most Water Authorities do understand that membership rolls are falling. Enough clubs have been disbanded under pressure of rising costs in recent years to make it clear that recreational boat owners are not to be regarded as a source of easy income for Water Authorities.

## 4. THE RIGHT TO LAY PERMANENT MOORINGS

Prima facie, ownership of the foreshore and of the seabed of tidal rivers and creeks is in the Crown, on the presumption that it is "waste of the Kingdom which has not been granted to another".

Equally, there is no doubt that there can be private ownership of the foreshore and of the seabed in tidal waters based on the proof or presumption of a grant from the Crown at some time or other, possibly in the remote past. There are numerous areas of salt water which are private property as a result of the granting of some ancient charter.

It has recently been established in the courts that there is (except in very particular and unusual circumstances) no Common Law right to lay or maintain permanent moorings in another person's land without his permission.

In *Fowley Marine (Emsworth) Limited v. Gafford* (1968) it was held that there is no common law right to lay or maintain permanent moorings, since "it would be little less than fantastic that, in the absence of statute or proved local custom, the law should allow anyone navigating a ship or vessel, including every amateur yachtsman, to place bulky objects on another person's land without permission and to retain them there, presumably forever, as being an ordinary incident of navigation."

In this relatively modern case, other points were discussed which are of interest. Under Section 4(1) of the Limitation Act 1939 an action may be brought by the Crown "at any time before the expiration of sixty years ..." in order to recover rights which may have been taken or claimed by another person or organisation.

Ordinarily, uninterrupted dispossession of the true owner's land for a period of twelve years or more would effectively debar the true owner from claiming back that land, but as against the Crown, the period is sixty years. It is however arguable that neither the Limitation Act 1939 nor case law has really established whether the act of laying and/or maintaining a permanent mooring can amount to dispossession of land. It remains uncertain whether a landowner (including the Crown) is, after the appropriate period, really barred from bringing an action to recover the land upon which the mooring lies, largely because of the difficulty of exact definition of the area of dispossession.

## 4.1 Methods of dispossession

As already stated, there is no common law right to lay or maintain permanent moorings on another person's land without his permission. Such a right may possibly be acquired by "lost modern grant" — a type of legal fiction which assumes that at some time in the past a document granting the right may have been in existence but has now been lost or forgotten.

A person may also seek to prove "custom", i.e. "everybody has done it over many years and nobody has complained".

The dispossession of the original owner's right may also be

given by statute. An example of this is the Water Act 1973 which gave to Regional Water Authorities considerable rights previously owned by others.

A person who lays or maintains a permanent mooring without permission may be a trespasser and accordingly liable to the owner of the seabed, river-bed etc. on or in which the mooring is placed.

## 4.2   A land owner's right to claim rent

In recent years a number of owners of "land covered by water" (however they acquire title) have insisted upon their proven right to claim rent for that area of land covered either by ground tackle or "sinkers".

This is the natural outcome of the changing nature of the yachting scene, the increasing number of people requiring moorings and the virtual chaos which has (or could have) arisen as a result of the assumption that a person may at will, without let, hindrance or permission, lay a permanent mooring in tidal water, since it appears to belong to nobody else.

## 4.3   Who can stop you laying a mooring in tidal water?

As mentioned above, the owner of the land covered by water can reasonably stop you from using his land upon which to lay a mooring. Other bodies may also be entitled to do so:

### 4.3.1   *Department of Transport*

Under Section 4 of the Coast Protection Act 1949 permission must be obtained from the Department of Transport before placing anything below the high-water mark which is, or may become, a danger to navigation. This includes mooring buoys.

### 4.3.2   *Crown Estate Commissioners*

Where land covered by tidal water apparently belongs to nobody, it almost certainly belongs to the Crown. Hence the Crown Estate Commissioners can exercise the rights of landlord and may withhold permission to lay a mooring until a rent has been agreed.

### 4.3.3   *Planning Authorities*

The laying of a mooring can sometimes amount to

"development". Within the jurisdiction of a Planning Authority, that Authority may restrain a person from laying a mooring by serving an Enforcement Notice. Local Government areas are fixed by the Local Government Act 1972 to a "medium" low-water mark; effectively this is the point of low-water at a date halfway between neap and spring tides. Such areas also include "accretions from the sea" and areas where the natural line of a watercourse has changed. The Town and Country Planning Act 1971 seems to follow the same "areas" and Planning Authorities therefore have powers above that same tide level. Below it, the sea is not subject to planning control.

Some time ago the RYA asked Counsel to give an Opinion on whether a Local Authority had power to serve an Enforcement Notice on a peson who had laid a mooring, on the basis that it amounted to an unauthorised development.

Counsel confirmed what we have said about the seaward boundary of the Local Authority and went on to discuss estuaries and arms of the sea. Whether an arm of the sea or a river is within the body of a county was considered in the case of *The Fagernes* (1972). The test was said to be whether a man on one shore could see what was done on the other. In that particular case it was probable that the river was within the parishes which formed the area of the administrative county for Local Government purposes. If the parish boundaries on either side of the river on 25 December 1968 did not extend to the middle of the river, they were (by the Poor Law Amendment Act 1868 — now repealed) extended to the middle of the stream. Counsel went on: "The onus of proof is on the person asserting that the land in question is within the county".

The recipients of a County Council notice were entitled to call on the County Council to prove that the land covered by water was within the County Council jurisdiction. If this proof was not forthcoming then the notices were null and void, ab initio.

Counsel also spoke of other aspects of the laying of moorings which might establish their permanence and therefore whether they amounted to "development". He discussed types of concrete blocks or discs with an anchor bar to which the mooring line is fixed and the usual practice of digging such moorings into the mud. He also referred to mooring bases which merely rest on the hard bottom. In either case, it was his view that development was involved within Section 22(1) of the Town and Country Planning Act 1971.

Counsel also remarked that the Minister had taken the view that the mooring of vessels (not in the course of navigation) is an operation in, over or under land. There might however be cases where if the mooring were not fixed or embedded, and was moved from time to time, then the laying of the mooring would not be a development operation since the act in question involves solely the use of a chattel. Thus it would be perfectly permissible to anchor a boat and leave it, provided it was not attached to a fixed mooring.

The mere fact that consent to lay a mooring has been obtained from the Harbour Authority or from the owners of the land did not, Counsel suggested, admit the need to obtain planning permission.

There are therefore two questions in each particular case which must be demonstrated by the facts:

(a) It must be established that the mooring is sufficiently permanent to be a true "development operation".

(b) It must be established beyond doubt that the Planning Authority has jurisdiction over the piece of land covered by water in which the mooring has been laid and over which the Council purports to have planning powers.

### 4.3.4 *Harbour and marina owners*

Harbour Authorities may derive their powers over harbour waters from Private Acts of Parliament or from the Harbours Act 1964 or a mixture of both. One of the many powers which they have is that of dictating what moorings may be laid and where. Marina owners, dependant upon the size of the marina, derive their powers from either a Private Act of Parliament or from some lease or licence accorded to them by the Crown Estate Commissioners, a Local Authority, or the Harbour Authority in which the marina is situated. They have the right to prohibit the laying of unauthorised moorings within their marina.

# VIII

# CHARITABLE STATUS

The question ofen arises as to whether some or all of the activities of a private, voluntary, members' club could be afforded charitable status.

"Charity" as generally understood differs from the way in which that word is used by lawyers who attach to it a meaning that is more easily expressed by a series of guiding principles rather than hard and fast rules.

The categories and purposes for which charitable status can be sought were defined in 1891 by Lord MacNaughten in the leading case of *Pemsel*. He said that as long as a trust was one which was set up for the public benefit, then those trusts which would qualify for charitable status would be those for:

(a) the relief of poverty;
(b) the advancement of education;
(c) the advancement of religion;
(d) other purposes beneficial to the community.

A "charity" if it complies with the definition of a trust (i.e. a legal device which enables one party (the settlor or donor) to settle a sum of money or property in the hands of another (the trustee) for the benefit of a third pary (the beneficiary)) is established by a particular form of what is known as an "express trust". The benefits which a charitable trust enjoys over and above those enjoyed by ordinary trusts are considerable, particularly in terms of tax concessions.

## 1. INCOME TAX

The scope of the income tax exemption basically provides that charities are exempt from tax on rents and other profits from land, tenements etc. vested in trustees for charitable purposes. By the same provision exemptions are applied to income derived from interest, annuities, dividends etc. subject to certain statutory conditions.

Exemptions are enjoyed in respect of trading income and one of the most important exemptions is for covenanted gifts of income. These arise where a person covenants to pay an income to a charity for a period of four years or more in which case the income becomes the income of the charity. Any annual payment which is part of the income of the charity is exempt from tax.

## 2.  CORPORATION TAX
A charitable corporation enjoys the same tax exemptions as trustees of a charity in relation to the income of the charity.

## 3.  CAPITAL GAINS TAX
A gain accruing to the charity which is applied for charitable purposes is exempt from Capital Gains Tax.

## 4.  INHERITANCE TAX
Gifts made more than seven years before the death of the donor are entirely exempt, otherwise exempt if amounting to less than £90,000.

## 5.  RATING RELIEFS
Charities have only enjoyed statutory relief from rates since 1955 as follows:
(a) Charities may claim from the relevant local authority a mandatory 50% relief from rates otherwise chargeable.
(b) Local authorities may in their discretion remit all or part of the balance of the general rate.

## 6.  CHARITY LAW AND SPORT
Institutions and trusts for the promotion of sport (or recreation in a wider sense) can qualify for charitable status in two ways. Firstly under the second or fourth heads in the *Pemsel* case refered to above, for the "advancement of education" or "other purposes beneficial to the community"; secondly under the Recreational Charities Act 1958.

Having said that, it is important to emphasise that a trust established for the promotion of sport is not charitable. In the case of *Re Nottage* (1895) a gift in the will of a former member of a yacht club provided for a cup to be donated to the club to be awarded as a prize in an annual competition. The stated object was to encourage the sport of yacht racing. The Court of Appeal held that "the encouragement of a mere sport or game, principally calculated to amuse individuals apart from the community at large, cannot be charitable, though such a sport or game is to some extent beneficial to the public".

In the House of Lords case of *Inland Revenue Commissioners v. McMullen* (1980) it was held that a trust for the promotion of sport which is independent of any educational institution can be charitable if it has an association with formal education because "no one of sense could be said to suggest that between these ages (10-19) any boy can be properly educated unless at least as much attention is given to the development of his body as is given to the development of his mind". The Lords have not extended this principle to adult education but young persons up to the age of 23 or so may benefit. The Lord Chancellor in the *McMullen* case said that "The legal conception of charity, and within it the educated man's ideas about education, is not static, but moving and changing — both change with changes in ideas about social values".

Thus the *Nottage* decision is reduced in significance and no longer bears on the use of funds connected with youth training. The *McMullen* case involved funds provided for the following purposes:

(a) To organise or provide facilities for football, or other games or sports in schools and universities and particularly:
   (i) sports equipment for the use of pupils;
   (ii) courses, lectures, demonstrations and coaching;
   (iii) provision of training colleges for sports teachers;
   (iv) provision of facilities, management and accommodation for games and sports.

(b) To organise and provide facilities for physical recreation in the interests of social welfare for boys and girls under 21 who, by reason of youth or social and economic circumstance, have need of such facilities.

As we have seen, charitable status can be obtained only by the formation of a trust with objects carefully drafted so that they fall within the test of a charity as extended by the *McMullen* decision. For example it is not sufficient for a club simply to say "we carry out training for boys and girls from the local comprehensive school". This does not constitute a charitable trust particularly if the other activities of the club are clearly non-charitable.

If a club is therefore able to hive off its youth training activities and has a surplus which is taxable, or investment income which is used for training purposes, registration of a charitable trust may be of benefit.

Some clubs whose membership is confined solely to children are registered as charities. Under the Recreational Charities Act 1958 the provision of recreational facilities is charitable if they are in the interests of social welfare, which is defined by the following test:

(a) The facilities are provided to improve the conditions of life for those using them; and

(b) Those persons have need arising out of youth, age, infirmity, disablement, poverty or social circumstance; or

(c) The facilities are available to the public at large or to women at large (an all-female club qualifies but not an all-male club).

# IX

# A SUMMARY OF STATUTE LAW
# AFFECTING CLUB-OWNED CRAFT

Although pleasure craft in this country are among the least regulated in the developed world, a number of Acts and Regulations do affect certain pleasure craft and pleasure craft used for certain purposes and this chapter covers the more important aspects of this body of legislation, as it relates to pleasure craft used for private purposes, chartering and teaching and to club launches and those in charge of such craft.

All Acts and Regulations mentioned below are available from HMSO, PO Box 276, London SW8 5AT, tel: 01 622 3316. Merchant Shipping Notices can be obtained from Marine Survey Offices.

## 1. PASSENGERS

Much depends upon the question of whether vessels are carrying "passengers". A passenger is defined as "any person not employed or engaged in any capacity on board on the business of the vessel (or travelling by reason of any circumstances which could not have been prevented, i.e. shipwreck) and not being children under one year of age". In a recent High Court case it was held that the term "engaged" implied the need for a binding contractual agreement, even though the person engaged may be unpaid or may even have paid the shipowner for the voyage.

*Merchant Shipping (Safety Convention) Act 1949*

## 2. PLEASURE YACHTS USED ENTIRELY FOR PRIVATE PURPOSES

2.1 All yachts over 13.7 metres (45ft) in length and those leaving British coastal water are required to be registered. In the case of yachts under 24 metres (79ft) the Small Ships Register is now available as a cheaper and simpler alternative to registration under Part I of the MSA 1894.

*Merchant Shipping Acts 1894 and 1983 and Merchant Shipping (Small Ships Register) Regulations 1983/1470.*

2.2   Notice of departure and arrival for and from abroad should be given to HM Customs and Excise using Form C1328.
*Pleasure Craft (Arrival and Report) Regulations 1979*

2.3   Owners or masters of pleasure craft over 80 tons GRT and 24 metres in length and sail training ships may be subject to regulations regarding the certification of deck officers unless eligible for exemption under Section 44 of the Merchant Shipping Act 1970.
*Merchant Shipping (Certification of Deck Officers) Regulations 1985/1306*

2.4   Pleasure yachts in Class XII (over 13.7 metres) are subject to life saving and fire appliance rules.
*Merchant Shipping (Life Saving and Fire Appliances) Regulations 1980-86.*

3.   **PLEASURE YACHTS LET ON CHARTER**
    Under Section 94 of the Public Health Acts Amendment Act 1907 (as amended) pleasure yachts let on charter may be required to be licensed. Licences are issued by the appropriate Local Authority (or, in a few special cases, under special Local Authority Acts). The present law applies throughout England and Wales by virtue of the Local Government Act 1972. The only craft requiring a licence are pleasure boats and vessels which are either (a) "let for hire to the public", or (b) "used for carrying passengers for hire". Persons in charge of navigation of craft used for carrying passengers for hire are also themselves required to be licensed (see "Boatman's Licences" below).
    In the view of the RYA, pleasure yachts let on charter are serviced by "crew" rather than "passengers". They will not therefore fall to be considered for licensing under (b) above. A yacht let to a friend or on a casual basis will not be "let for hire to the public" but yachts which are regularly advertised for charter will be so let.
    The letting of a private yacht (i.e. parting with possession temporarily) will require a licence only if there is a commercial element (i.e. some pecuniary reward is envisaged) and the yacht is let to the public (eg. by advertisement rather than purely as a private arrangement). Any arrangement between a member of an unincorporated club and the club

will not amount to "a letting for hire", as it falls within the definition of mutual trading.

## 4. CLUB LAUNCHES

Club launches are affected by the Merchant Shipping Acts 1894, 1964, 1970 and 1979, the Merchant Shipping (Safety Convention) Act 1949 and the Public Health Acts Amendment Act 1907. Those who "drive" them may be required to have a DTp or other "licence" (see "Boatman's Licences" below).

It is clear from existing case law and the statutes that club launches cannot be said to be carrying only crew. Most of those on board must be described as "passengers" for they are in no way working the ship.

### Survey

(a) More than 12 passengers:

Launches carrying more than twelve passengers must be surveyed (Section 271 MSA 1894 as amended by Section 17 MSA 1964). Apply for Form Survey 6 from your local Department of Trade Marine Survey office if your club is operating such a vessel. The requirements are stringent and may prohibit a petrol driven engine.

Launches carrying more than twelve passengers are subject to these regulations whether or not they are "let on hire to the public" and whether or not "passengers" have paid money. Section 94 of the Public Health Acts Amendment Act 1907 specifically exempts vessels which are already "licensed" by the Department of Transport and thus vessels with passenger certificates do not need a Local Authority licence under Section 94.

(b) 12 or less passengers:

Club launches carrying twelve or fewer passengers will only require a Local Authority licence if they are "let on hire to the public" or are "used for carrying passengers for hire". If the service is provided free or is merely reflected in general club membership fees then the vessel will not be subject to the statute for there is no element of "hire to the public" or "carrying passengers for hire". Such vessels are not subject to DTp survey.

## 5. TEACHING ESTABLISHMENTS

The RYA takes the view, and this has been accepted by

Local Authorities in England at least, that pleasure yachts used for training are not "let for hire to the public" since the payment relates to the tuition being received. Equally those on board are "crew" and such vessels cannot be said to be "carrying passengers for hire".

Hence, the RYA is of the opinion that such vessels do not fall to be licensed under Section 94 of the Public Health Acts Amendment Act 1907.

## 6.  BRITISH WATERWAYS BOARD AND OTHER INLAND NAVIGATION AUTHORITIES

As mentioned above, Section 94 applies to pleasure boats and vessels which are "let for hire to the public" or "used for carrying passengers for hire". Section 94 has now been amended so that no licence will be required under that Section for pleasure boats and vessels whilst on any canal owned or managed by the British Waterways Board even though they are "let for hire to the public" or "carrying passengers for hire". Such vessels remain subject to the Board's own requirements as to registration, construction and use.

The Board, the Anglian Water Authority and the Thames Conservancy are three authorities which presently demand vessels on their water to conform with their regulations as to construction and use. No doubt in the future there will be other authorities controlling inland waterways which produce their own special construction and use regulations. Unfortunately there is no common code and each authority has its own special quirks hidden within its regulations. If you are buying a vessel specifically for use on a particular waterway you are advised to check the regulations before you purchase.

## 7.  LOAD LINE REGULATIONS

The Merchant Shipping (Load Lines) Act 1967 applies to all ships except ships of war, ships solely engaged in fishing and pleasure yachts. There is often some doubt as to whether the owners of certain types of pleasure craft require exemption from the provisions of the Act. The RYA takes the view that a pleasure yacht, whether or not it is engaged in trade, remains a pleasure yacht and is therefore outside the provisions of the Act and the owner need not even consider obtaining a Load Line Exemption Certificate.

## 8.  BOATMAN'S LICENCES

Merchant Shipping Notice No M1036 to owners and persons in charge of small passenger vessels is issued by the Department of Trade and applies to club launches.

To ensure the safe handling of such vessels which carry limited numbers of passengers and which ply in smooth or partially smooth waters or go only short distances to sea, the DTp will issue Boatmen's Licences to persons suitably qualified. So far as club launches are concerned, the Notice applies to Class IV and V vessels carrying not more than 250 passengers. A candidate for a Boatman's Licence must be eighteen or over, must not be suffering from any disease or disability which could make it unsafe for him to be in charge of a passenger vessel, and must pass an eyesight test and an oral test in practical seamanship and local pilotage. This test will include manoeuvering, rules of the road, use of life-saving equipment and fire-fighting appliances, knowledge of fire precautions and weather reporting systems and an oral test on local pilotage (eg. knowledge of the coastline, buoys, tidal streams etc.)

Those holding Second Mate, Mate (Home Trade), Second Hand, a Class V Certificate under the Merchant Shipping (Certification of Deck Officers) Regulations 1980, DoT Yachtmaster (Coastal), or an RYA Coastal Skipper Certificate or higher will not be required to undergo these tests. Application forms can be obtained from any Marine Office.

The licence will be restricted to the area in which the holder has passed a test of local pilotage or produced evidence to show that he has adequate experience. Club launches may legally carry more than twelve passengers only in accordance with the limits shown on the Passenger Certificate and persons in charge of such vessels should therefore hold a Boatman's Licence valid for the limits within which the vessel is employed.

Certain Local Authorities and Harbour Authorities issue their own Boatman's Licences and require all passenger vessels plying within their areas to carry a licensed boatman. Possession of a DTp Boatman's Licence will not relieve the holder from complying with any legal requirements of such Local or Harbour Authority.

## 9.  LOG BOOKS

The requirement imposed by Section 68 of the Merchant Shipping Act 1970 that an official logbook shall be kept in every ship registered in the United Kingdom shall not apply to:

(a) a ship belonging to a general lighthouse authority;

(b) a ship of less than 25 gross tons; or

(c) a pleasure yacht.

*Merchant Shipping (Official Log Books) Regulations 1981/569*

## 10.  POWERS OF DISTRICT COUNCILS TO LICENSE VESSELS

In 1972 District Councils were required to operate Section 94 of the Public Health Acts Amendment Act 1907 but many District Councils have not appreciated this fact and have no licensing system. If you do require a licence the District Council may charge an appropriate fee and impose conditions. Such conditions will relate to the protection of the hirers or passengers (as the case may be) for that is the only purpose of the section. Some District Councils have attempted to impose Load Line Certification together with burdensome survey requirements and restraints on areas of operation and length of passage. These are generally outside the scope of the powers of Section 94 and may be objected to for that reason.

*Local Government Act 1972*

## 11.  CLASSIFICATION OF SHIPS

For the purposes of the Merchant Shipping Acts, all ships are classified. Club launches are likely to be considered under Class IV or V. Pleasure yachts over 13.7 metres (45ft) LOA are normally classed under Class XII. It is a matter of debate whether Class XI "Sailing Ships" embraces Sail Training Ships. The full classification is as follows:

| | |
|---|---|
| Class I | Passenger ships engaged on voyages (not being short international voyages) any of which are long international voyages. |
| Class II | Passenger ships engaged on voyages (not being long international voyages) any of which are short international voyages. |
| Class II(A) | Passenger ships engaged on voyages of any kind other than international voyages. |

| | |
|---|---|
| Class III | Passenger ships engaged only on voyages in the course of which they are at no time more than 70 miles by sea from their point of departure and not more than 18 miles from the coast of the United Kingdom, and which are at sea only in fine weather and during restricted periods. |
| Class IV | Passenger ships engaged only on voyages in partially smooth waters, or in smooth and partially smooth waters. |
| Class V | Passenger ships engaged only on voyages in smooth waters. |
| Class VI | Passenger ships engaged only on voyages with not more than 250 passengers on board, to sea, in smooth or partially smooth waters, in all cases in fine weather and during restricted periods in the course of which the ships are at no time more than 15 miles, exclusive of any smooth waters, from their point of departure nor more than 3 miles from land. |
| Class VI(A) | Passenger ships carrying not more than 50 passengers for a distance of not more than 6 miles on voyages to or from isolated communities on the islands or coast of Scotland, and which do not proceed for a distance of more than 3 miles from land. |

Ships other than passenger ships:

| | |
|---|---|
| Class VII | Ships (other than ships of Classes I, VII(A), VII(T), X, XI and XII) engaged on voyages any of which are long international voyages. |
| Class VII(A) | Ships engaged in the whaling industry or employed as fish processing or canning factory ships, and ships engaged in the carriage of persons employed in the whaling, fish processing or canning industries. |
| Class VII(T) | Tankers engaged on voyages any of which are long international voyages. |
| Class VIII | Ships (other than ships of Classes II, VIII(T), IX, X, XI and XII) and other ships engaged only on voyages which are not international voyages. |
| Class VIII(A) | Ships (other than ships of Classes II(A) to |

95

VI(A) inclusive, VIII(A)(T), IX, IX(A), X, XI and XII) and other ships engaged only on voyages which are not international voyages.

| | |
|---|---|
| Class VIII(A) (T) | Tankers engaged only on voyages which are not international voyages. |
| Class IX | Tugs and tenders (other than ships of ClassII, II(A), III, VI and VI(A)) which proceed to sea but are not engaged on long international voyages. |
| Class IX(A) | Ships (other than ships of Classes IV to VI inclusive) which do not proceed to sea. |
| Class IX(A) (T) | Tankers which do not proceed to sea. |
| Class X | Fishing vessels other than ships of Classes I to VI(A) inclusive. |
| Class XI | Sailing ships (other than fishing boats and ships of Class XII) which proceed to sea. |
| Class XII | Pleasure craft (other than ships of Classes I to VI(A) inclusive) of 45 feet in length or over. |

# X

# FINANCIAL ASSISTANCE

Apart from the obvious solution of a bank loan, clubs needing to raise a capital sum have various possible sources of funds:
1. Sports Council
2. Local Authority
3. English Tourist Board
4. European Community Loans
5. Brewery
6. Internal, i.e. their own members
7. Sponsorship or patronage

## 1. SPORTS COUNCIL

A grant or loan may be offered towards the reasonable capital cost of providing facilities for those taking an active part in sport. No assistance can be offered towards the cost of routine maintenance or repairs or for the replacement of equipment. Facilities which can be assisted are:
(a) Indoor sports facilities such as sports halls, ancillary halls and their associated changing rooms.
(b) Outdoor sports facilities such as pitches, courts, floodlighting, and their associated changing rooms.
(c) Specialist facilities such as gymnastic halls, rifle ranges and launching slipways.
(d) Purchase of land and sporting rights.
(e) Purchase of sports equipment:
   (i) Where the equipment is an integral part of the development of a new facility.
   (ii) New major items of equipment with a total capital cost in excess of £1,500.
(f) Special facilities for disabled people which meet all the following qualifications:
   (i) Not sited at a hospital or special school for the disabled (but exceptions may be considered by the Sports Council where adequate community use of the facility is assured).

(ii) Primarily recreational rather than therapeutic.

(iii) Not capable of being provided by sharing general community provision for similar activities.

(g) Provision of social accommodation to complement an existing sports facility (eligible only for loan).

The number of eligible projects seeking assistance is always more than the available funds will satisfy. In the selection of applications to be offered assistance, priority will be given to those which will best achieve the aims of the Sports Council by increasing participation, improving performance or helping to alleviate social or recreational deprivation in areas of special need.

## 1.1 Amount of grant and loan

The contribution of the Sports Council will be at the level considered necessary to ensure that the project will be completed satisfactorily. The level of assistance to be offered will be individually assessed for each project, taking account of the financial need and the resources available to the applicant. Local Authorities are also empowered to assist voluntary organisations with the development of facilities and the Sports Council requires applicants to seek assistance from their Local Authority at the earliest opportunity.

The Sports Council scheme is subject to the following limits:

(a) A grant will not exceed 50% of the approved cost of the project (except in areas of special need where the limit is 75%).

(b) A loan will not exceed 50% of the approved cost of the project and the maximum loan is £10,000.

(c) Where both grant and loan are given, the combined total will not exceed 75% of the approved cost of the project.

(d) The total grant contribution from public funds (eg. Local Authority, Manpower Services Commission, Sports Council) will not exceed 75% of the approved cost of the project. (However, in areas of special need, any contribution from the Local Authority will not count against this limitation).

(e) The minimum grant is £750 (minimum project cost £1,500).

(f) The minimum loan is £1,000 (minimum project cost £2,000)

(g) For the purchase of property (land/buildings) or sporting rights, the approved cost will be the valuation of the District Valuer if this is lower than the actual cost.

## 1.2 Conditions

There are certain conditions which the Sports Council is required to attach to grants and loans in order to safeguard the use of public funds. Applicants will be required formally to accept and comply with these conditions which are set out below.

*Conditions applying to both grants and loans:*

(a) The application must be made on behalf of a voluntary organisation not constituted or operated for profit for its members and there must be no provision for the distribution of assets or funds to members or other persons during the existence of the organisation or its dissolution.

(b) There must be evidence of financial need, i.e. that the organisation could not provide the proposed facility without the aid of a grant or loan.

(c) Membership of the organisation must be open to all and no application for membership refused on other than reasonable grounds, eg. there must be no discrimination on grounds of creed, colour, religion or political persuasion. Any ballot for the admission of members must be decided by a simple majority vote.

(d) The managing body of the organisation must be composed mainly of members representing those using the facilities, with all active adult members eligible for election to the managing body.

(e) The organisation must have security of tenure on the facilities (including playing facilities) either through the ownership of the freehold or by means of a satisfactory lease for a period of 28 years. In certain cases a lesser period will be accepted but the level of grant or loan will be limited as follows:

| Security of tenure Years | Max: Grant/Loan £ |
|---|---|
| 21 | 15,000 |
| 14 | 10,000 |
| 7 | 5,000 |

(f) The organisation must not have committed itself by

purchase, contract or other binding agreement to the project for which assistance is sought and must not do so in advance of a written offer of grant or loan from the Sports Council unless prior written consent is obtained.

(g) The organisation must be able to meet at least 25% of the capital cost from non-statutory sources.

(h) The organisation, at the time of application, must be able to demonstrate to the satisfaction of the Sports Council its ability to meet the balance of the capital cost of the project, the cost of adequately maintaining the facility after completion and the cost of the loan repayments where appropriate.

(i) The facility will be adequately insured.

(j) The Sports Council will have the right of access and inspection of the facility.

(k) The books and accounts of the organisation will be made available if required for examination by the Sports Council.

(l) The Sports Council may make any further conditions it considers necessary. These conditions will be set out at the time the offer is made.

*Additional conditions applying to grants only:*

(a) The property of the organisation must not be subject to a mortgage or loan exceeding 25% of the cost of the project. Secured loans in excess of 25% will be allowed only where the body making the loan is prepared to give an undertaking to the Sports Council guaranteeing the continued use of the facility for sports purposes approved by the Sports Council or the repayment of the grant in the event of foreclosure.

(b) The Sports Council will be entitled to withhold payment of the grant (or any part thereof) and require immediate repayment of advances made if the grant is not applied to carrying out the project, or if the project is not completed to the satisfaction of the Sports Council.

(c) If the grant-aided facility is disposed of, or ceases to be used for sports purposes approved by the Sports Council, or if any of the other conditions of grant are not met, the organisation will be required to repay to the Sports Council an appropriate proportion of the grant or the market value of the facility.

*Additional conditions applying to loans only:*
(a) There must be no constitutional restriction on the organisation borrowing up to the amount of the loan.
(b) The organisation will be responsible for any stamp duties and legal costs incurred by the Sports Council in respect of the loan.
(c) The Sports Council will be entitled to withhold payment of the loan (or any part thereof) and require immediate repayment of advances made if:
    (i) The loan is not applied to carrying out the project, or the project is not completed to the satisfaction of the Sports Council.
    (ii) The borrower disposes of an interest in the project.
    (iii) The facility ceases to be used by the borrower for the purpose for which the loan was given.
    (iv) The borrower does not comply with the method and terms of repayment agreed with the Sports Council.
(d) Loans must be secured by personal guarantors or by Local Authority guarantee. Personal guarantors should not normally exceed ten in number and bank references will be taken up by the Sports Council in respect of each guarantor.
(e) Loans will be interest free, repayable in ten equal half-yearly instalments over five years by Banker's Order.

### 1.3 Sports participation grants

The Sports Council also gives grants towards innovatory schemes which will encourage and increase participation in sport. These grants are mainly for non-capital items concerned with the development of sport. Allowable costs include coaches' costs/fees and facility hire charge and administration. Grants may also be considered towards capital expenditure on sports equipment and modest building projects with a cost not exceeding £3,000 when they are undertaken as part of a scheme to promote participation.

### 2. LOCAL AUTHORITY

There is little in the realm of recreation and leisure which Local Authorities are not empowered to provide for, such as sports, recreation, playing fields etc. However, unlike housing, education and similar services there is very little that they are required to do. Their powers are discretionary and, unfortunately for yachting, we have an undeserved reputation as a wealthy sport, so it is an uphill task to get anything out of the majority of Local Authorities. However, there are precedents. The RYA itself, when it was promoting the National Yacht Racing Centre at Weymouth, secured the promise of substantial grants from the Sports Council and both district and county councils. Advice on Local Authority aid can be obtained from the local Director of Leisure Services (titles may vary, but this is the usual one in England). Clubs are,however, advised to consult their Regional RYA Committee at an early stage.

## 3.  REGIONAL TOURIST BOARD

The Regional Tourist Boards have a general remit to promote facilities in any area whereby facilities or attractions for visitors are improved. In theory this can extend to the provision of visitors' berths at a yacht club marina development, or of shoreside facilities.

## 4.  EUROPEAN COMMUNITY

The Commission of the European Communities, although having no funds available *per se* for the provision of sporting facilities, is able to assist in the provision of facilities to the extent that the European Regional Development Fund can assist tourist projects if they are sited in assisted areas. These are designated by the Department of Trade and Industry and are largely in Scotland, the North, the West Midlands and Wales. A marina is given by their Grants and Loans Information Officer as an example of an eligible project if sited in such an area.

## 5.  BREWERY

For those clubs which have a bar, a local brewery may easily be prepared to make a loan at very reasonable rates for improvement to the bar itself, the club lounge or the catering facilities in return for a commitment to buy supplies solely from the brewery concerned. The drawback to this arrangement is that the magistrates responsible for registration of the club may object, and require the club to obtain a liquor licence with its more demanding requirements.

## 6. INTERNAL FUND RAISING

### 6.1 Bonds

Some clubs have successfully raised substantial capital from their own members by issuing bonds. For example, a club wishing to raise £2,400 repayable over 5 years would issue 60 bonds of £40 each to members secured on the club's assets. Bonds are redeemed for £50 and 15 are drawn each year for 4 years. The 15 members who are lucky enough to be included in the first draw make a handsome profit and even the last 15 have some increase to offset against inflation. The club has had to pay a total of £600 in interest charges over the 5 years which is less than would normally be charged by a bank. There are obviously many variations on this theme. Most clubs will be able to work out a variation to suit their particular needs, but further advice from the RYA can be obtained if needed.

### 6.2 Interest-free debentures issued by an incorporated club

In seeking loans from members, for which no interest is to be paid, clubs should be careful not to imply that membership subscription fees will be waived since VAT is payable on subscriptions. It may, however, be that the club is prepared to suffer the VAT as a small interest payment on a loan which otherwise attracts no interest payment. It is not recommended that unincorporated clubs issue any sort of unsecured interest-bearing or interest-free loan notes. These should only be issued by trustees who will be personally liable even if club assets should be insufficient. The form of loan note which appears at Appendix 8 relates to a loan made by a member of a club who does not expect to receive interest.

Other sorts of debentures may be issued at a fixed interest rate based on the going rate in the market or in certain cases issued without interest but with some service being provided to the holder of the debenture note which he would not otherwise obtain as a normal club member. Professional advice should be obtained to determine the conditions of issue and repayment of these debentures. They should carry no additional voting rights and the conditions should provide safeguards against debenture holders demanding immediate repayment which might cause problems for the club. You may also have to consider your club constitution in connection with the possible cessation of the club (though this eventuality is covered in the draft form set out at Appendix 8).

## 7. SPONSORSHIP OR PATRONAGE

Some large companies are prepared to help yacht clubs, especially those situated in the neighbourhood of their premises, particularly if one or more of the directors are yachtsmen. Even when no outright grant is obtainable it may be possible to get help in return for some limited publicity for the company's name or the name of one of its products. Clearly the recent Rule 26 relaxations give increased scope for this sort of activity.

# XI

# CLUB MAGAZINES

(A "Media Guide" to a club's relations with the press
is included at Appendix 6.)

## 1.  LIBEL

Any club or class association publishing a newsletter or
magazine, particularly if it is lively and controversial, will
inevitably have cause from time to time to make a judgement
as to whether to print, amend or withdraw a personal or
professional comment likely to affect the reputation of some
inidividual, firm or company.

Libel is defined in this context as the publication of
defamatory matter in writing.

Defamation is the making of a statement that reflects on
the personal character, reputation, office or vocation of the
victim. So far as personal character is concerned the test of
defamation is whether the statement is likely to lower the
plaintiff in the estimation of right-thinking members of
society generally, or would cause him to be shunned or
avoided.

## DEFENCES TO LIBEL

### 1.1  Justification

Clearly a plea of justification should not be entered until
the defendant has clear evidence to support the claim. If a
club magazine intends to discredit, for example, a local yacht
broker or boatyard it would be as well to have details of at
least two or three hard cases, complete with witnesses who
will be prepared to appear for the defence, before venturing
into print. So often a complaint by one individual member
may be found on close examination to lack real substance and
a defamatory article based on such a complaint may land the
editor and the club in trouble.

### 1.2  Fair comment

Fair comment and criticism on matters of public interest
are protected, even though the character of an individual may
suffer. To fall within the defence of fair comment the

statements complained of must be published honestly as criticism and as the real opinion of the speaker or writer and not from some malicious motive. In fact, in both "fair comment" and "qualified privilege" cases, the motive of the person publishing the remark is all-important. However, in cases of criticism of artistic or literary works (and that includes sailing books) it is open to the critic to be as withering as he pleases, so long as he is not activated by an improper motive. If a book is dreadful, badly written and a waste of money, then the law takes the view that the critic should not be circumscribed in his right to say so. Even gross exaggeration will not make a comment unfair. However wrong a comment may be, or however prejudiced the writer, it may still be within the prescribed limit, so long as it is not perversely unjust.

The right to comment is not limited to literary or artistic works. The public acts of a public person (eg. a local councillor, or a harbour commissioner) may be made the subject of fair comment by all members of the public. Where there are untrue allegations of alleged misconduct, the defence does not apply. Where the alleged libel consists partly of statements of fact and partly of statements of opinion based on those facts, those facts must be substantially true in order to support a defence of fair comment. Private institutions on the other hand may not be made the object of protected public comment; a local newspaper article regarding a club commodore's incompetence would not therefore be protected, but a club magazine's remark may be protected under the defence of qualified privilege.

### 1.3 Qualified privilege

This arises where the author of the statement has an interest or a legal, social or moral duty to make it known to the recipient, who himself has a corresponding interest or duty in receiving it. For the defence to succeed the defendant must show:

(a) that the occasion was fit;

(b) that the statement had reference to the occasion; and

(c) that the statement was published from right and proper motives.

Examples of qualified privilege are the compiling of a staff report or reference or a relevant and necessary article in a house magazine or a letter from a tenant to co-tenants about the landlord. It is an essential ingredient of the defence that the information or statement is necessary for the information of recipients, and for the guidance and regulation of their conduct. If the communication cannot influence conduct, then there is no privilege. The defence is available even where a wide publication has been made; an MP giving public political advice to all his constituents has been held privileged.

## 1.4 Unintentional defamation

Under Section 4 of the Defamation Act 1952 there is a procedure whereby in cases of unintentional and non-negligent defamation within the limits of the section a defendant may avoid liability to pay damages if he is willing to publish a reasonable correction and apology and to pay the plaintiff's reasonable costs and expenses.

The section only applies to words published innocently, in that the publisher did not intend to libel the victim or that the words were not obviously libellous but had a hidden meaning of which the publisher was ignorant, and that in either case he exercised all reasonable care in relation to the publication.

The publisher may make a statutory "offer of amends" which will mean offering to publish an apology and correction, and as far as possible distributing the apology and correction to the recipients of the original libel.

A statement will only be libellous if it is untrue but even if the statement may be true, it will be a brave editor who prints seriously critical material in his magazine unless he is prepared, and has the resources, to defend a libel action.

## 1.5 Statutory defence

In an action for a libel contained in any public newspaper or periodical the defendant may plead that it was inserted without malice and without gross negligence, and that as soon as the facts were brought to his attention he inserted at the earliest opportunity a full apology, or if the periodical appeared less than once a week, had offered to publish an apology in any newspaper or periodical selected by the plaintiff. Payment into court must also be made of an unspecified sum, which is a matter of judgement for the defendant.

If the offer of amends is accepted, the victim cannot thereafter take legal action. If the offer is rejected and legal action taken, the defendant may raise the question of the offer in his defence. The offer will be a complete defence if the defendant can show it was reasonable, was not delayed, and that the statement complained of was not made maliciously.

## 2.  COPYRIGHT

The editor of a club or class magazine will often wish to reprint reports or articles of interest published in the commercial yachting press. As a rule it should always be assumed that a magazine's proprietors enjoy the copyright of any magazine article or report. Accordingly an unauthorised publication or copying of such an article is likely to constitute a breach of copyright. By the same token most magazines will be only too pleased to give their consent to the reprinting of an article provided that the reprint is courteously attributed to the magazine in question.

Breach of a copyright, or failure to comply with a condition attached to consent to reproduce will give rise to a cause of action for damages and injunction. It pays (and requires very little effort) to keep in with the yachting press.

# XII

# TAXATION

## 1. INCOME TAX

Throughout the legislation imposing taxation in the UK, reference is made to the word "person". "Person" includes a body of persons corporate or unincorporate and references in the legislation to a person should therefore be read as referring to an association or club.

In law an unincorporated association has no legal existence separate from that of its members and in each case the tax authorities will look at each club to determine how the finances are controlled and how the body is organised, inspecting the constitution to see exactly where the liability for tax (if any) should fall.

Whether a body is corporate (for example a company limited by guarantee) or an unincorporated association makes no difference for tax purposes. "Company" for income and corporation tax purposes means a body corporate or an unincorporated association. A company resident in the United Kingdom is subject to corporation tax on its total worldwide profits which comprise both income and capital gains. A company is resident in the UK if the central management and control of the company is exercised here, regardless of the place where it is incorporated or legally constituted. To ascertain where control and central management of the company is exercised, the Inland Revenue would have regard to where management meetings are held and the residence of those who would be regarded as directors if the association were a corporate body.

There are no special rules or concessions for bodies which promote sport or recreation unless they are charities. Sports clubs may therefore receive income from any of a wide variety of sources including Sports Council grants and at the same time be liable for corporation tax on their surplus and on their investment income.

Foreign income is taxed as it arises in a similar way to UK income but a credit against corporation tax payable is allowed for foreign income taxes paid. This credit is limited to the UK tax actually charged on that foreign income.

Corporation tax is charged at the rate of 29% on companies where profits are below £100,000 in a year and marginal reliefs apply to profits between that figure and £500,000. Above that level the full rate of 35% applies. A deduction of 1/7th is allowed from capital gains and the balance is charged to corporation tax at the full rate of 35%, producing an effective rate of tax on gains of 30% whether or not the lower corporation tax rate applies to other profits. Corporation tax is normally payable 9 months after the end of the accounting period or, if later, 30 days after the issue of an assessment. Associations established prior to 1965 may have a longer interval between the end of their accounting period and the normal date of payment. Interest on overdue tax is charged and is not tax-deductible.

Associations which carry on trade to finance other activities are liable to corporation tax on the profits from trading. They are also liable to tax on interest and investment income. Dividends from UK companies are not subject to corporation tax (since they are paid out of income which has already been charged to corporation tax). Income from land is also assessable as are gains on disposals of investments and other chargeable assets.

## 1.1 Mutual trading

If a body of persons carrying on a trade does so in such a way that the members of the body and the customers are one and the same, any profit arising is not subject to tax. Such a profit is regarded as the members' own money and thus returnable to them. Membership subscriptions of an association are generally taxable but there is no liability to tax in respect of profits made from members who avail themselves of the facilities provided for them. An association or club is assessable to tax on profits derived from trading with non-members.

## 1.2 Fund raising and sponsorship

Sponsorship money often has strings attached. Some advantage is obtained by the sponsor (usually publicity) and thus he is able to claim a deduction for the money given. The recipient is not taxed on the amount received unless it can be said to be a profit from a trade or an annual profit or gain.

Provided no service is accorded and the sponsorship income is purely passive it is not subject to tax.

Likewise income from lotteries is not subject to tax unless it arises from a trade. The Inland Revenue may contend in individual cases that income from lotteries conducted by clubs and associations represents trading profits.

## 1.3  Charities

A body of persons or trust established for charitable purposes only (whether or not registered as such with the Charity Commissioners) enjoys almost complete exemption from taxes on income and capital gains. Trading income is subject to tax unless the trade is exercised in the course of carrying out a primary purpose of the charity or if the work in connection with the trade is carried out by the beneficiaries of the charity. Where this does not apply, the trade can be conducted by a company which covenants its income to the charity thereby avoiding corporation tax on the income. There is a concession which prevents profit from jumble sales etc. from being taken into account for tax purposes unless the charity trades regularly.

## 2.  VALUE ADDED TAX

VAT is charged on the supply of goods and services in the UK in the course or furtherance of a business, and on the importation of goods into the UK whether or not for business purposes.

The provision by a club or association of the facilities or advantages available to its members in return for a subscription or other consideration is deemed to be the carrying on of a business. Also the admission, for a consideration, of persons to any premises by such organisation is deemed to be the carrying on of a business.

VAT is charged on the supply of goods and services in the UK if it is a taxable supply and is made by a taxable person. A taxable person is one who is or should be registered for VAT purposes. An association or club which is treated as carrying on a business and makes taxable supplies (eg. most subscriptions, mooring fees, etc.) is required to register for VAT purposes if the value of those supplies exceeds £21,300 in any 12 month period or has exceeded £7,250 in the previous calendar quarter. Registration is usually backdated in the case of a failure to register and VAT is payable whether or not it has been charged to members or customers.

It is the joint and several responsibility of the Chairman (or Commodore) Secretary and Treasurer of an association or club to notify HM Customs and Excise of liability to register for VAT. This must be done on the official form at the beginning of a year in which taxable supplies are expected to exceed £21,300.

All taxable supplies must be aggregated to see whether the registration threshold has been reached. Where for example teas or drinks are sold in the club room, takings must be added to subscriptions, as must mooring fees, dinghy park fees etc. (but not race entry fees which are specifically exempted under the 1980 Competitions Exemption Order).

## 2.1  Taxable supplies

Supply for VAT purposes includes all forms of supply and transactions such as sales, winnings and performance of services including the granting, assignment or surrender of a right for a consideration. In the case of an association or club the facilities available to members are treated as a supply for this purpose. Such supplies are subject to VAT at the standard rate of 15% unless specifically exempted or zero-rated. Subscription income of a youth club is exempt, as is the income of any club where the only benefit is a book or magazine (and where a magazine or book is one of a number of benefits, a pro-rata reduction in VAT is allowed). Where a club finances out of its subscription income activities which are designed to benefit the public at large as much as its own members, an appropriate part of each subscription can be regarded as a donation and outside the scope of VAT.

Income from sponsorship is a supply where there is a supply of services or the granting of a right in the course or furtherance of a business. Where a sponsor is given the right to display his name or product that is a supply for VAT purposes. This would probably be regarded as the provision of advertising services and would therefore be zero-rated if provided to a person who "belongs" abroad.

## 2.2  Input tax

All clubs suffer VAT on purchases of goods and services. An association which is registered is able to recover tax suffered on supplies purchased for the purposes of the business it is deemed to carry on. In effect it is able to recover input tax on supplies purchased for the provision of facilities to members. As a first step in calculating recoverable input tax it is necessary to consider what facilities and advantages are provided to members in return for subscriptions. The next step is to see whether or not the goods or services on which VAT was charged were supplied to the club. The final question is whether the goods were for the purposes of the provision of facilities to members.

## 2.3  VAT Accounts

Every taxable person must maintain such records as the VAT Commissioners may require. There is no prescribed form, but the records must contain sufficient information accurately to identify taxable transactions, both inputs and outputs.

The standard accounting period is 3 months, but for smaller traders (i.e. up to £100,000 turnover per annum) a 12-month period with 9 equal monthly payments and a 10th balancing payment has recently been introduced.

## 2.4  Zero-rated supplies

These include books, booklets, pamphlets and leaflets, journals and periodicals and transport of passengers in vehicles and ships designed or adapted to carry at least 12 (eg. a club-operated coach or launch). Food and drink are not zero-rated if supplied in the course of catering nor if the drink is subject to duty.

## 2.5  Exempt supplies

Insurance, the right to enter a competition, the provision by a youth club of facilities available to its members are all exempt supplies.

## 3.  RATING OF CLUB PREMISES

There are four essential ingredients to rateable occupation:
(a) There must be actual occupation or possession.
(b) Occupation must be exclusive for the particular purposes of the possessor.
(c) Possession must be of some value or benefit to the possessor.
(d) Possession must not be for too transient a period.

The unit of assessment for rating purposes is the hereditament. In most cases this will include land and buildings, and rates will be payable on all land (not just buildings) including land covered by water. For a hereditament to be rateable it must be clearly definable. In one case a golf club had a licence to use an undefined area of the New Forest as a golf course and it was held for this reason that the club was not in rateable occupation of that area.

The hereditament must also be capable of separate occupation. Thus a sailing club sharing with others similar rights over the water it uses for its activities should not be liable to rates. If the club has an exclusive right for its purposes over a particular defined area of water, that area probably will be rateable.

### 3.1 Person liable for rates

In most cases under the Rates Act the rateable person is not the owner but the occupier. In the case of a club having a freehold or lease the trustees in whose name the property is vested will bear the primary liability for payment of rates. In the case of a club having no more than a licence to use premises and facilities it is unlikely that such use will amount to rateable occupation.

### 3.2 Gross, net annual and rateable values

The rates raised by the Rating Authority are levied by reference to the rateable value of the hereditament, the amount payable being a multiple of the rate levied for that year and the rateable value of the premises. The appropriate rateable value is calculated by reference to a hypothetical rent which might reasonably be expected to be obtained on an annual letting. The essential difference between the figures is that for the purposes of the gross value the landlord is assumed to bear the cost of repairs, insurance and maintenance generally, while for the rateable value the tenant is assumed to do so.

### 3.3 Moorings and floating vessels

It has long been established that the use of land for moorings, or for the anchoring of floating vessels, docks or pontoons, can, if the necessary conditions are satisfied, give rise to rateable occupation. In particular such use must be sufficiently permanent.

Whether the mooring, vessel or pontoon is rateable depends on the use to which it is put, what shore services are laid on (eg. mains, electricity, telephone, water etc.) the period of mooring (whether for days, months or years at a time) and whether, in the case of a vessel, it is built or adapted for use in navigation or for use as a houseboat.

The rating of moorings received specific attention in the passage of the Rates Act 1985. At the suggestion of the Royal Yachting Association the Government agreed to bring the law on mooring rates into line with that in Scotland. In particular, any mooring is now exempt from rates if:

(a) it is used or intended to be used by a boat or ship; and
(b) it is equipped only with a buoy attached to an anchor, weight or other device:
    (i)  which rests on or in the bed of the sea or any river or other waters when in use; and
    (ii) which is designed to be raised from the bed from time to time.

This in effect means that all "swinging" moorings of the conventional type are exempt, whether secured by a single block, anchor or weight, or attached to a ground chain, or to a series of anchors, provided that they are designed to be raised for renewal or inspection from time to time.

Also exempt are fore and aft moorings of the same general design as swinging moorings, where the yacht has a buoy at each end.

Not exempt, clearly, are driven-pile and screw-pile moorings, other permanently fixed and bank-side moorings.

The Rates Act 1985 also enables Valuation Officers to assess individual moorings collectively to enable Local Authorities to serve rates demands on the authority controlling and receiving the fees for moorings. This will only apply to fixed moorings (eg. piles, marinas, river bank moorings etc.) but will transfer to the authority controlling the harbour responsibility for collecting a contribution to the total assessment from each of the mooring holders.

This method of collection should result in lower rates liabilities than would otherwise arise through individual demands. The authority responsible for the payment of rates must, if requested by the occupier of a mooring, supply information to enable the occupier to calculate his proportion of the total rate liability based on information provided by the Valuation Officer. Any occupier of a rateable mooring may apply to have his mooring separately assessed.

115

### 3.4 Principles of valuation

The valuation list is compiled and assessed by the Valuation Officer, subject to a number of principles laid down by the courts:

(a) Each hereditament must be independently assessed.

(b) The hereditament to be valued must be assumed to be vacant and to let.

(c) Every intrinsic quality and circumstance which tends to increase or decrease the value must be taken into consideration.

(d) The hereditament must always be "the actual house or other property for the occupation of which the occupier is to be rated and is to be valued rebus sic statibus" (as it stands). It is therefore not to be rated by reference to its value as structally altered or put to some different mode of use.

(e) The value arrived at should represent "the figure at which the hypothetical landlord and tenant would come to terms for that hereditament on the open market".

(f) The actual rent at which a hereditament is let or at which other similar hereditaments are let is not necessarily conclusive evidence but may be the best evidence of value.

In the context of sailing clubs which are purpose-built for the storage and repair of boats and tackle it is reasonable to assume that when the premises are valued it should be on the basis of their being let for their present use as sailing club premises and for the repair and storage of sailing equipment. However, club premises often incorporate a bar and other recreational, non-sailing, accommodation. In such cases the Valuation Officer may argue that the rateable value should be assessed as if the premises were a social club rather than a sailing club. Such an argument might well increase the rateable value. Much depends on the premises, but the argument would be wrong in principle in the following cases:

(a) Where the premises were purpose-built or altered and used for the purpose of wholly or mainly storing and repairing boats, the administration of a sailing club and for sailing activities including showering and changing.

(b) Where the club premises (whether used for social purposes or not) form part of a larger rating assessment which includes the water used by the club.

(c) Where the club was able to obtain two separate rating assessments for its premises. One for the bar etc. and one for that part used solely for sailing purposes.

Where club premises are used mainly for social activities, clubs may expect a higher rating assessment. This method of valuation would be appropriate if the hypothetical use by the social club could be effected without structural alteration and without any material change in the mode of use.

In the case of *Sussex Motor Yacht Club Ltd v. Eilmore* (1966) the Lands Tribunal held that the premises could only be let for boating purposes and not for purely social club purposes. The clubhouse was modern and purpose-built and contained changing rooms, a boat store and club offices in addition to club rest rooms and a bar. The clubhouse was also in a commercial harbour. As a result of its particular facts this case cannot be used as a general proposition that all sailing clubs must be rated as though they could only be used for sailing club purposes. The club argued that the clubhouse could only be used by the existing club and that accordingly the rent (and therefore the rateable value) would be fairly low. The Valuation Officer argued that the club was not the only possible tenant. If the club moved, other boating clubs might be interested and accordingly the rateable value should be assessed by reference to rateable values of similar premises in nearby areas. This argument was upheld.

### 3.5 Appeals

Those aggrieved may at any time make proposals for alteration of the valuation list in connection with that hereditament. The grievance might relate to the inclusion of the hereditament in the list, the values contained in the list, or the valuation in the list as a single hereditament of a building or a portion of a building occupied in parts. A Valuation Officer may also make proposals for any alteration of entries in the list.

Where either the occupier or the Valuation Officer objects to the proposal, an objection must be lodged within 28 days of service of the proposal, the case is then heard by the local valuation panel, with a right of appeal to the Lands Tribunal provided that, for an appeal to lie, the aggrieved party must have had appeared before the local valuation panel.

Appeals on points of law only lie from the Lands Tribunal to the Court of Appeal. In the event of any procedural irregularity there is a right of appeal to the High Court.

### 3.6  Rate relief

Section 40 of the Rates Act 1967 provides two useful reliefs, one discretionary and one obligatory. In the case of a registered charity it is entitled by virtue of Section 40(1) to a reduction of one half of the rates otherwise chargeable.

Under Section 40(5) the rating authority is given a discretion to reduce or remit the payment of rates chargeable in respect of various hereditaments including any other hereditament which is occupied for the purposes of a club, society or other organisation not established or conducted for profit and which is wholly or mainly used for the purpose of recreation.

The exercise of this discretionary relief varies from one Local Authority area to another depending on a number of factors. So long as sailing maintains its image as an exclusive sport for the wealthy, a major determining factor will be the political complexion of the Local Authority. Experience indicates that clubs which play a real part in the local community, perhaps making their facilities available to schools, youth groups, sea scouts etc., holding open days and generally keeping in contact with councillors and council officers are very much more likely to attract rating relief. However, unless a particular council can be shown to have acted in a wholly malicious or arbitrary way, the High Court (which has a general jurisdiction to review all administrative acts by public bodies) will not interfere. From time to time over the years various sports bodies have aired the possibility of legislating to compel Local Authorities to grant relief but such ideas have never gained sufficient support.

# APPENDIX 1

# ABANDONED BOATS
# ON CLUB PREMISES

The problem frequently arises where, for any one of a number of reasons, the committee of a club finds itself having to deal with a dinghy that has been apparently abandoned in the dinghy park, or a boat that has been left on its moorings for a long period of time, there being no trace of the former club member responsible for the boat.

Although the boat in question may be an eyesore, unless it has actually become a nuisance or a danger, those who interfere with it do so at their peril if the owner has paid all requisite storage, parking or mooring charges.

In the absence of any club rule covering abandoned boats, where the committee has ascertained that charges have been unpaid for some time, they should adopt the procedure laid down in Schedule I of the Torts (Interference with Goods) Act 1977:

1. Attempt to trace the owner by all reasonable means, eg. attaching a notice to the boat in a weathertight envelope in a prominent position, posting a notice on the club board soliciting information from the members as to the whereabouts of the owner and following up leads or information that may be forthcoming. The notice should identify the boat in question, state that it must be removed and specify the sum payable by the owner to the club by way of arrears of mooring charges.

2. If the committee fails to trace the owner having taken all reasonable steps to do so, then they are entitled to sell the goods, having first attempted to notify the owner.

3. A notice of intention to sell the goods shall:
   (a) Specify the name and address of the club and identify the boat in question and where it is lying;
   (b) Specify the date on or after which the committee intends to sell the boat;
   (c) Specify the amount which is payable by the owner in respect of the boat and which became due before the giving of the notice.

The notice must be served in reasonable time before the proposed sale and, if a sum of money is due, not less than 3 months beforehand. The notice should be sent by registered letter or recorded delivery to the last known address of the owner.

4. The sale must take place at the best possible price. It would be as well to advertise the sale reasonably widely and a record of all advertising and of the details of the sale should be kept for 6 years, lest in years to come the owner should reappear and claim that the sale was 'rigged' at an artificially low price.

5. The proceeds of the sale, after the deduction of legal costs, costs of sale, mooring charges and any others attributable to the boat in question, should be calculated and minuted by the committee. The proceeds should be deposited in a bank and retained against the eventuality of a claim by the owner within a period of 6 years for the net proceeds together with accrued interest.

The committee should consider introducing a new general rule. Despite the fact that a person may no longer be a member, the rules amount to a contract between the club and each individual member and there is no reason in principle why certain rights and obligations under the contract should not continue, even after the expulsion or retirement of a member.

It is suggested that a new general rule should be included on the following lines:

"If at any time any mooring fees payable to the club by any member or former member shall be three months or more in arrears:

(a) The committee shall be entitled to move the boat to any other part of the premises without being liable for any loss of or damage to the boat howsoever caused.

(b) The committee shall be entitled upon giving one month's notice in writing to the member or former member, at his last known address shown in the register of members, to sell the boat and to deduct any monies due to the club (whether by way of arrears of subscriptions or mooring fees or otherwise) from the net proceeds of sale before accounting for the balance (if any) to the member or former member.

(c) Alternatively any boat which in the opinion of the committee cannot be sold may, upon such notice as aforesaid, be disposed of in any manner the committee may think fit and the expenses recovered from the member or former member. Any arrears as aforesaid shall be deemed to be a debt owing to the club by the member or former member.

(d) Further the club shall, at all times, have a lien over members' or former members' boats parked or moored on the club's premises or club moorings in respect of all monies due to the club, whether in respect of arrears of mooring fees or subscriptions or otherwise.''

### Registered boats

If the boat is registered under the Merchant Shipping Act, title to it can be transferred only by Bill of Sale or following arrest and sale by order of a competent Court of Admiralty jurisdiction. The club can not therefore pass good title under the rules set out above. In these circumstances it is up to the purchaser to satisfy himself, by enquiring of the Registrar of Ships at the yacht's Port of Registry, that the club has the right to sell the boat and that the boat is free of charges, mortgages etc. Having bought the boat he will then be in a position to apply for "closure" of the registration under the provisions of the 1983 Merchant Shipping Act and to re-register (through the RYA) on the Small Ships Register.

### Hire Purchase agreements

The boat may be the subject of a hire purchase agreement in which case the actual owner of the boat would be the hire purchase company. That company would have a right of action against the club, if the club were to sell the boat under the rules set out above.

Assuming that the club sells the boat for a proper price, the result will merely be that the club would have to pay over the proceeds to the hire purchase company, rather than to the former owner. However the club would probably find itself having to pay the hire purchase company's legal costs in addition and there could be adverse publicity.

### Boat owned by a member under eighteen years of age

Special rules apply to contracts made by minors and a club should seek legal advice if it wishes to dispose of a boat believed to belong to a minor.

121

## Strict adherence to the club rules

If the club wishes to exercise its powers under the suggested rule it must be absolutely certain that it has complied with the strict letter of the rule. When dealing with what is, in effect, a penal provision, the courts incline to resolve any questions of doubt (such as ambiguities in the rule or defects in procedure) in favour of the individual rather than the club.

## Effective deterrents

The club may consider two courses of action in anticipation of the problem of abandoned boats:

1. It may insist on payment of a deposit by a member who wishes to take up a berth or hard standing. The deposit would have to be reasonably substantial if it were to be an effective deterrent.
2. Under the last part of the proposed rule, the club obtains a "lien", that is to say the club can refuse to deliver up the boat to the owner until he has discharged all monies due to the club.

# APPENDIX 2

# SPECIMEN SET OF RULES FOR A YACHT CLUB

The model rules are divided into the following sections:
1. Name amd Objects
2. Officers
3. Membership
4. Management Committee
5. Trustees
6. Meetings of the Club
7. Dissolution of the Club
8. Byelaws etc.

NOTE
1. Where a club sells or supplies intoxicating liquor, clauses marked with an asterisk * must be included to satisfy the requirements of the Licensing Act.

2. Where words are enclosed in square brackets they may be omitted as required or, where alternatives are offered, amended to suit the special requirements of a club.

3. When amending any rule to suit a particular club's purpose, care should be taken that such amendment does not vary the meaning or intent of any other rule.

4. The side-headings are provided for convenience and do not affect the meaning of any clause.

## SECTION 1 — Name and Objects
1. The name of the club shall be "The . . . . . . . . . . Club" (hereinafter referred to in these rules as "the club").

2. The object for which the club is formed is to promote and facilitate the sport of yachting and also to provide social and other facilities for members as may be from time to time determined.

## SECTION 2 — Officers

Officers of
the club

*3.  The Officers of the club shall be Full or Family members of the club and shall consist of a Club President,[ ] Vice-Presidents, a Commodore, a Vice-Commodore, a Rear-Commodore, [an Honorary Secretary and an Honorary Treasurer]. Officers shall be elected at the Annual General Meeting in each year and shall hold office for one year, retiring at the termination of the Annual General Meeting in each year. All Officers of the club shall be eligible for re-election.

4.  The [Honorary] Secretary (and/or the Assistant [Honorary] Secretary) shall:

Duties of
Honorary
Secretary

(a)  Keep a register of club members' names and addresses;

(b)  Conduct the correspondence of the club;

(c)  Keep custody of all club documents;

(d)  Keep full minutes of all meetings of the club, the committee and sub-committees which shall be confirmed and signed by the appropriate chairman upon the agreement of the club, the committee or sub-committee at the next following meeting of the club, the committee or sub-committee;

(e)  Administer such insurance policy or policies as may be needed fully to protect the interests of the club, its officers and its members.

(f)  Maintain contact with the club's legal adviser to ensure that the club's affairs are managed in accordance with current law.

Duties of
Honorary
Treasurer

5.   The [Honorary] Treasurer shall:

(a)   Cause such books of account to be kept as are necessary to give a true and fair view of the state of the finances of the club.

(b)   Cause all returns as may be required by law in relation to such accounts to be rendered at the due time.

(c)   *Prepare an Annual Balance Sheet as at [    ] in each year and cause such Balance Sheet (and accounts as necessary) to be audited at least once annually and shall thereafter cause the same to be exhibited in the club premises at least fourteen days before the date of the Annual General Meeting.

6.   The Honorary Auditors shall:

(a)   be appointed at the Annual General Meeting in each year [and shall be two appropriately qualified members of the club];

Duties of
Honorary
Auditors

(b)   audit the accounts of the club when called upon to do so and give such certificate of assurance as to the accuracy of the said accounts as shall be required by law or by the committee;

(c)   if either is unwilling or unable to act, inform the committee who shall appoint a substitute to hold office until the termination of the next Annual General Meeting.

## SECTION 3 — Membership

Categories
and votes
of
membership

7.   There shall be the following categories of membership with power to vote at all meetings of the club as indicated hereunder. The rights and privileges of each category of members are as defined in the latest edition of the byelaws of the club.

A FULL MEMBER — being a person who, at the date of election, is over the age of eighteen shall have one vote.

A FAMILY MEMBER — which expression shall include one or two parents (as may be) and all children under eighteen years of age. The family unit shall have one vote, exercisable by either parent.

A JUNIOR MEMBER — being a person who, at the date of election, is under the age of eighteen shall have no vote. Such a member shall be one who at the commencement of the subscription year joins the club other than as a full member or a family member.

AN HONORARY MEMBER — who shall be nominated and elected in the manner described in Rule 46 shall have one vote.

A SOCIAL MEMBER — who shall have no vote.

A TEMPORARY MEMBER — who shall have no vote.

No member except a Temporary Member may use the club premises, or any of the facilities of the club until forty-eight hours have elapsed from the date of posting of notice of election.

*Candidates for membership shall have no privileges whatsoever in relation to the use of the club or premises.

Membership Entrance & Subscription Fee

8. The rate of Entrance and Subscription Fee for each category of Membership shall be proposed by the committee to the members at the Annual General Meeting in each year. Any proposed changes shall be approved by a majority of those present and entitled to vote and

shall become operative on the first day of January in the year following. The current rate of Entrance and Subscription Fee shall be prominently displayed in the club premises.

9.  Members shall also make the following annual payments:

(a)  An annual boat permit fee of such a sum as the committee shall from time to time prescribe which shall entitle a member to [sail his or her own boat on the water controlled by the club/a space in the club's boat park].

(b)  Such an annual sum as shall from time to time be demanded to defray the club's subscription to the RYA as a Fully Affiliated club.
All members shall pay the Entrance Fee (if any) and their first annual subscription upon election to the club and thereafter on the first day of January in each year: Provided that a member elected after the first day of June in any year shall pay half the annual subscription applicable for that year and that a member elected after the first day of November in any year shall not be required to pay any subscription in respect of the year of election, but shall pay, on election, the Entrance Fee and the annual subscription in respect of the year following election.

10.  Every member shall furnish the [Honorary] Secretary with an up-to-date address which shall be recorded in the Register of Members and any notice sent to such address shall be deemed to have been duly delivered.

## Election and retirement of members

Candidates
for election

11. Every candidate for membership (except candidates for Honorary Membership) shall be proposed and seconded for election by a Full or Family member of the club, both of whom must be personally acquainted with the candidate.

Application
for
membership

12. An application for membership shall be in the form from time to time prescribed by the Committee and shall include the name, address and occupation of the candidate, and the signatures of the Proposer and the Seconder.

Election of
members

*13. Upon receipt of an application for membership, the [Honorary] Secretary shall enter such application in a Register of Candidates and shall cause the application form to be prominently displayed in the club premises for at least [fourteen] days before the meeting of the committee at which such application for membership shall be considered. The election of all classes of members is vested in the Management Committee and shall be by a simple majority vote of those members present and voting at the relevant meeting of the Management Committee. The [Honorary] Secretary shall inform each candidate in writing of the candidate's election or non-election. He shall furnish an elected candidate with a copy of the Rules and Byelaws of the club and make request for such payments as are necessary.

Payment of
fees upon
election

14. Upon election, a candidate shall pay, within one calendar month, such entrance and other fees as shall be requested. In default of such payment, the election shall be void unless

sufficient cause for delay be shown.

| | |
|---|---|
| One year's temporary absence of member | 15. A member who, for any reason, anticipates inability to use the club or its facilities for the whole of any one year shall be excused payment of the annual subscription and other annual fees provided that notice in writing is given to the [Honorary] Secretary before the last day of November in the previous year. A member wishing to be re-instated during the year in question shall pay such portion of the annual subscription as the committee shall require. |
| Retirement of a member | 16. A member desirous of retiring from membership shall give notice in writing to the [Honorary] Secretary before the last day of November and shall not then be liable to pay the subscription for the following year. Upon re-application by a past member the committee may, at its discretion, excuse the payment of an Entrance Fee. |
| Arrears of subscription | 17. The committee may cancel, without notice being given, the membership of any member whose annual subscription and other annual fees are more than three months in arrears provided that the committee may, at its discretion, re-instate such member upon payment of arrears. No member whose annual payments are in arrears may enter any club event or regatta nor vote at any meeting. |

## Conduct of members

| | |
|---|---|
| Undertaking by members to comply with rules | 18. Every member, upon election and thereafter, is deemed to have notice of, and impliedly undertakes to comply with, the club Rules and the current Byelaws and Regulations of the club. |

**Expulsion of members**

Any refusal or neglect to do so, or any conduct which, in the opinion of the committee, is either unworthy of a member or otherwise injurious to the interests of the club, shall render a member liable to expulsion by the committee.

PROVIDED THAT, before expelling a member, the Committee shall call upon such member for a written explanation of the member's conduct and shall give the member full opportunity of making explanation to the committee, or of resigning.
A resolution to expel a member shall be carried by a simple majority vote by those members of the Management Committee present and voting on the resolution.

**Guests in the club**

19. Members shall enter the names of all guests in the Visitor's Book. Not more than three guests may be introduced in any one day and the same guest may not be introduced more than six times in any calendar year.

**Damage to club property**

20. A member shall not knowingly remove, injure, destroy or damage any property of the club and shall make restitution for the same if called upon to do so by the committee or by the [Honorary] Secretary upon the instructions of the committee.

**Exhibiting of notices**

21. A member shall not cause any communication in whatever form to be exhibited on club notice boards or premises without permission of the [Honorary] Secretary.

**Settlement of accounts**

22. A member shall settle any indebtedness for refreshment or otherwise before leaving the club premises, or in

accordance with any byelaw relating to the settlement of such indebtedness.

Suggestions

23. All suggestions shall be entered in the Suggestion Book and signed by the Member.

Complaints

24. Complaints of any nature relating to the management of the club premises shall be addressed in writing to the [Honorary] Secretary. Under no circumstances shall a servant of the club be personally reprimanded by a member.

Members of other RYA clubs

25. A member of any club affiliated to the Royal Yachting Association (a list whereof is published by the said Association) may be authorised to use the premises of the club by any member of the committee of the club. Such authorisation shall specify between which dates (not being more than fourteen days apart) the said person may so use the premises.

Competitors in club races

26. Any person who is a competitor or crew member in any race sponsored by or on behalf of the club is entitled to the use of the club premises and to purchase intoxicating liquor for consumption on the premises by such person or his guest, within a period of 24 hours before and after the race in which they are competing.

Power to expel those admitted under rules 25 & 26 hereof

27. The [Honorary] Secretary or any other person who has received the authority of two members of the committee, may expel, temporarily or permanently, any person who has the right to the use of the club premises only under rules 25 and 26.

**Limitation of club liability**

28. Members, their guests and visitors are bound by the following Rule which shall also be exhibited in a prominent place within the club premises:

Limitation
of club
liability

Members of the club, their guests or visitors may use the club premises, and any other facilities of the club, entirely at their own risk and impliedly accept that:

(a) The club will not accept any liability for any damage to or loss of property belonging to members, their guests or visitors to the club.

(b) The club will not accept any liability for personal injury arising out of the use of the club premises and any other facilities of the club either sustained by members, their guests or visitors or caused by the said members, guests or visitors whether or not such damage or injury could have been attributed to or was occasioned by the neglect default or negligence of any of them the Officers, committee or servants of the club.

**SECTION 4 — Management Committee**

Constitution
of Committee

*29. The Management Committee (herein referred to as 'the Committee') shall consist of the Officers, ex officio, and not less than [four] nor more than [eight] Full or Family members of the club elected at the Annual General Meeting each year to hold office until the termination of the next following Annual General Meeting.

Retirement
of members
of the
Committee

30. At the Annual General Meeting each year two of the Full and Family members shall retire in order of election or seniority. In the case of equal

132

seniority the order of retirement shall, failing agreement between the members concerned, be determined by lot. Members retiring under this rule shall not be eligible for re-election to the Committee until the Annual General Meeting next following the meeting at which they retire.

Candidates for election to Committee

31. Candidates for election to the Committee (not being Officers of the Club) shall be those members of the retiring Committee eligible to offer themselves for re-election and such other Full or Family members whose nominations (duly proposed and seconded in writing by Full or Family members of the club) with their consent shall have been received by the [Honorary] Secretary at least twenty eight days before the date of the Annual General Meeting in each year. Such nominations, together with the names of the proposer and seconder shall be posted in the club premises at least fourteen days prior to the date of the Annual General Meeting.

Election of Committee by ballot

32. If the number of candidates for election is greater than the number of vacancies to be filled then there shall be a ballot.

No contest for election

33. If the number of candidates for election is equal to or less than the number of vacancies to be filled then all candidates shall be deemed to be elected if two thirds of those present at the Annual General Meeting, and entitled to vote, vote in favour of such election.

Equality of votes

34. In the event of the ballot failing to determine the members of the Committee because of an equality of votes the candidate or candidates to be elected from those having an equal

133

number of votes shall be determined by lot.

| | |
|---|---|
| Casual vacancy | 35. If, for any reason, a casual vacancy shall occur, the Committee may co-opt a Full or Family member to fill such a vacancy until the next following Annual General Meeting. |

Retiring Commodore ex officio

36. A retiring Commodore shall serve as an ex officio member of the Committee in the year immediately following his retirement.

Committee meetings

37. The Committee shall meet at least every two months making such arrangements as to the conduct, place of assembly and holding of such meetings as it may wish. The Commodore or in his absence a Chairman elected by those present shall preside.

Voting at Committee

38. Voting (except in the case of a resolution relating to the expulsion of a member) shall be by show of hands. In the case of equality of votes the Commodore or Chairman (as the case may be) shall have a second and casting vote.

Quorum

39. Five members personally present shall form a quorum at a meeting of the Committee.

**Powers of the Committee**

Management of club by Committee

*40. The Committee shall manage the affairs of the club according to the Rules and shall cause the funds of the club to be applied solely to the objects of the club or for a benevolent or charitable purpose nominated by General Meeting.

Powers to make Byelaws and Regulations

41. The Committee shall make such Byelaws and Regulations as it shall from time to time think fit and shall cause the same to be exhibited in the club premises for fourteen days before the date of

implementation. Such Byelaws and Regulations shall remain in force until approved or set aside by a vote at a General Meeting of the club.

Appointment of sub-committees

42. The Committee may appoint such sub-committees as it may deem necessary and may delegate such of its powers as it may think fit upon such terms and conditions as shall be deemed expedient and/or required by the law. Such sub-committees shall consist of such members of the Committee or of the club as the Committee may think fit. Officers of the club shall be ex officio members of all such sub-committees.

Disclosure of interest to third parties

43. A member of the Committee, of a sub-committee or any Officer of the club, in transacting business for the club, shall disclose to third parties that he is so acting.

Limitation of members' liability

44. The Committee, or any person or sub-committee delegated by the Committee to act as agent for the club or its members, shall enter into contracts only so far as expressly authorised, or authorised by implication, by the members. No one shall, without the express authority of the membership in General Meeting, pledge the credit of the membership.

Members' indemnification of Committee

45. In pursuance of the authority vested in the Committee by members of the club, members of the Committee are entitled to be indemnified by the members of the club against any liabilities properly incurred by them or any one of them on behalf of the club wherever the contract is of a duly authorised nature or could be assumed to be of a duly authorised nature and entered into on behalf of the club.

The limit of an individual member's indemnity in this respect shall be a sum equal to one year's subscription at the then current rate for that category of membership unless the Committee has been authorised to exceed such limit by a General Meeting of the Club.

Nomination of Honorary Members by Committee

*46. The Committee may nominate for election at an Annual General Meeting such Honorary Members as the Committee may think fit. The total of such Honorary members shall not, however, at any time, exceed five percent of the total number of members nor shall the number of Honorary Members exceed at any one time six in number.

The election of Honorary Members shall be put to the vote at the Annual General Meeting each year and such Honorary Members shall be duly elected if two thirds of those present, and entitled to vote, vote in favour of election.

**Purchase and supply of excisable goods**

Purchase and supply of excisable goods

*47. The purchase for the club of excisable goods and the supply of the same upon club premises shall be exclusively and solely under the control of the committee, or of a special sub-committee appointed by the Committee.

Intoxicating liquor may only be sold for consumption on the club premises to persons over the age of eighteen who are entitled to the use of the club premises in pursuance of the Rules, Byelaws and Regulations for the time being in force. No Junior Member under the age of eighteen may purchase or attempt to purchase intoxicating liquor within the

136

club premises nor may a Junior Member under the age of sixteen purchase or attempt to purchase tobacco or cigarettes within the club premises.

**Hours of sale of excisable goods**

*48. Subject to the requirements of the licensing authorities, the Committee shall cause the club bar to be opened at convenient times (and such times shall be prominently exhibited in the club premises) for the sale of excisable goods to persons who are entitled to the use of the premises of the club in pursuance of these rules (except Junior Members as aforesaid): PROVIDED THAT visitors' names and addresses and the name of their introducer shall have been entered in the Visitor's Book upon entry to club premises.

**Profits from sale of excisable goods**

*49. No person shall take a commission, percentage or other such payment in connection with the purchase of excisable goods for the club. Any profit deriving from the sale of such goods shall (after deduction of the costs of providing such goods for the benefit of the club) be applied to the provision of additional amenities or the purchase of property to be held in trust for the benefit of the club.

**Accounts relating to excisable goods**

*50. Proper accounts of all purchases and receipts shall be kept and presented at the Annual General Meeting in each year and such information as the [Honorary] Secretary or [Honorary] Auditors may require shall be furnished to enable any statutory return or statement and the payment of excise or other duty or tax to be made.

## SECTION 5 — Trustees

Number of
and terms
of reference

51.  There shall be at least three Trustees of the club who shall be appointed from time to time as necessary by the Committee of the club from among Full, Family or Honorary Members who are willing to be so appointed. A Trustee shall hold office during his lifetime or until he shall resign, by notice in writing given to the Committee, or until a resolution removing him from office shall be passed at a meeting of the Committee by a majority comprising two-thirds of the members present and entitled to vote.

Property of
club vested
in Trustees

52.  All property of the club, including land and investments, shall be held by the Trustees for the time being, in their own names so far as is necessary and practicable, on trust for the use and benefit of the club. On the death, resignation, or removal from office of a Trustee, the Committee shall nominate a new Trustee in his place, and shall as soon as possible thereafter take all lawful and practicable steps to procure the vesting of all club property into the names of the Trustees as constituted after such nomination. For the purpose of giving effect to any such nomination, the [Honorary] Secretary for the time being is hereby nominated as the person to appoint new Trustees of the club within the meaning of Section 36 of the Trustee Act 1925 and he shall by deed duly appoint the person or persons so nominated by the Committee.

Powers of
Trustees

53.  The Trustees shall in all respects act, in regard to any property of the club held by them, in accordance with the directions of the Committee, and shall have power to sell, lease, mortgage or

pledge any club property so held for the purpose of raising or borrowing money for the benefit of the club in compliance with the Committee's directions (which shall be duly recorded in the minutes of the proceedings of the Committee) but no purchaser, lessee or mortgagee shall be concerned to enquire whether any such direction has been given.

**Indemnity of Trustees from club funds**

54. The Trustees shall be effectually indemnified by the Committee out of the assets of the club from and against any liability, costs, expenses and payments whatsoever which may be properly incurred or made by them in the exercise of their duties or in relation to any property of the club vested in them, or in relation to any legal proceedings, or which otherwise relate directly or indirectly to the performance of the functions of a Trustee of the club.

## SECTION 6 — Meetings of the club

**Annual General Meeting**

55. An Annual General Meeting of the club shall be held each year in the month of [November] on a date to be fixed by the Committee. The [Honorary] Secretary shall at least fourteen days before the date of such meeting or of any General Meeting as hereinafter mentioned post or deliver to each member notice thereof and of the business to be brought forward thereat.

**Business at Annual General Meeting**

56. No business, except the passing of the accounts and the election of the Officers, Committee, Trustees and Honorary Auditors, and any business that the Committee may order to be inserted in the notice convening the meeting shall be discussed at such meeting unless notice thereof be given in writing by a member entitled to vote to

the [Honorary] Secretary at least forty two days before the date of the Annual General Meeting.

**Special General Meeting**

*57. The Committee may at any time, upon giving twenty one days notice in writing, call a General Meeting of the club for any special business, the nature of which shall be stated in the summons convening the meeting, and the discussion at such meeting shall be confined to the business stated in the notice sent to members.

**General Meeting upon request of members**

*58. The Committee shall similarly call a General Meeting upon a written request addressed to the [Honorary] Secretary by at least [   ] members. The discussion at such meeting shall be confined to the business stated in the notice sent to members.

[Note to Clause 58. For the purposes of the Licensing Act 1964 this Clause must be limited to a maximum of thirty members OR 1/5th of the total membership, whichever is less]

**Chairman at meetings**

59. At every meeting of the club the President or the Commodore or, in their absence, a Chairman elected by those present shall preside.

**Quorum at meetings**

60. [Fifteen] members entitled to vote and personally present shall form a quorum at any meeting of the club.

**Entitlement to vote at meetings**

61. Only Full, Family and Honorary members shall vote at any meeting of the club. Other members may attend but are not entitled to vote.

**Voting at meetings**

62. Voting, except upon the election of members of the Committee shall be by show of hands.

Equality of
votes

63. In the case of an equality of votes the Chairman shall have a second or casting vote, on any matter other than the election of members of the Committee.

Voting on
rule change

64. On any resolution properly put to a meeting of the club relating to the creation, repeal or amendment of any Rule, Byelaw or Regulation of the club such Rule, Byelaw or Regulation shall not be created, repealed or amended except by a majority vote of at least two-thirds of those present and entitled to vote.

## SECTION 7 — Dissolution of the club

65. If, upon the winding up or dissolution of the club, there remains after the satisfaction of all its debts and liabilities any property whatsoever, the same shall not be paid to or distributed amongst the members of the club but shall be given or transferred to some other institution or institutions having objects similar to the objects of the club, such institution or institutions to be determined by the members of the club by resolution passed at a General Meeting at or before the time of the dissolution and if and so far as effect cannot be given to such provision then to some charitable object.

## SECTION 8 — Byelaws

Rights and
privileges
of members

i. The present rights and privileges of each category of membership shall be as follows:

A FULL MEMBER shall have the full use of all the club facilities.

A FAMILY MEMBER, his/her spouse and all children under the age of eighteen shall have the full use of all the

141

club facilities subject only to Rule 47.

A JUNIOR MEMBER shall have the full use of all the club facilities subject only to Rule 47.

AN HONORARY MEMBER shall have the full use of all the club facilities.

A SOCIAL MEMBER shall have the full use of the club-house facilities.

A TEMPORARY MEMBER (which expression may include members of another RYA affiliated club or organisation) shall have the full use of the club facilities but:

(a) Shall have no right to enter club races or regattas unless specifically authorised by the Honorary Secretary or Committee.

(b) Shall have no right to introduce visitors to the club or the facilities thereof.

(c) Shall have no right to take any part in the management of the club.

(d) Is deemed to have notice of and impliedly undertakes to comply with the club Rules, current Byelaws and Regulations as if he or she were a member of the club and so far as the said Rules, Byelaws and Regulations may be deemed to apply to such Temporary Member.

(e) Shall be liable to expulsion from the club premises or prohibited from using club facilities if, in the opinion of the [Honorary] Secretary, he or she shall not have reasonably complied with the above conditions.

Control of dogs   ii. No dogs may be brought into club premises.

| | |
|---|---|
| Admittance of children | iii. Children under fourteen years of age may only be admitted to the club premises for the service of food. |
| Control of car parking | iv. Cars may only be parked in areas designated for such parking so as not to cause an obstruction to other cars or to the approaches to the club premises. |
| Opening of club premises | v. The club premises shall be open to members at such times as the Committee shall direct. The present hours of opening are as follows: |
| Permitted hours for the sale of intoxicating liquor | vi. The permitted hours for the sale of intoxicating liquor are as follows:<br>Monday — Thursday   [          ]<br>Fridays and Saturdays   [          ]<br>Sundays, Good Friday and Christmas Day                       [          ]<br>and the bar will be open at these hours or at such other hours as may be decided by the Committee subject to any restrictions imposed from time to time by the Licensing Justices. |
| Abandoned boats | vii. In addition to the powers given to the Committee under Rule 17 and Rule 41 hereof if, at any time, any fees payable to the club by any member or former member shall be three months or more in arrears and a vessel the property of a member of former member remains upon the club premises, the Committee may: |
| | (a) Move the vessel to any other part of the club premises without being liable for any loss or damage to the vessel howsoever caused. |
| | (b) Give one month's notice in writing to the member or former member at his last known address as shown in the Club Register and thereafter sell the vessel and deduct any monies due to the club |

143

(whether by way of arrears of subscription or annual payments, mooring, dinghy park fees or otherwise) from the net proceeds of sale before accounting for the balance (if any) to the member or former member.

(c)   Alternatively, if the vessel is unsaleable, after giving notice in writing as aforesaid, dispose of the vessel in any manner the Committee may think fit and deem the cost of doing and any arrears as aforesaid to be a debt owing to the club by the member or former member.

PROVIDED ALWAYS THAT:

Proper evidence is available to show that all reasonable steps have been taken to trace a member or former member and that when and if the vessel is sold the proceeds of sale (less any indebtedness by the member or former member to the club) shall be placed upon bank deposit account and retained against the eventuality of a claim by the owner (whether he be the said member or former member or otherwise) for a period of six years.

# APPENDIX 3

# AGREEMENT FOR THE CHARTER OF A PLEASURE CRAFT

An abbreviated form of agreement prepared by the RYA for the use of club-owned yachts going foreign.

AN AGREEMENT made the day of 19
BETWEEN:- ("the Owner")
of
and of
of
of
of
("the Hirer/s")

In respect of the charter of the UN/REGISTERED PLEASURE CRAFT

Name:

Description:

Including all equipment machinery and gear on board ("the Yacht") and any specific inventory attached hereto initialled by both parties and forming part of this agreement.

DEFINITIONS

| "Charter Period" | : | from | hours on | 19 |
| | | to | hours on | 19 |
| "Cruising limits" | : | the area bounded by | | |
| "Charter Fee" | : | the sum of £ | | |
| "Owner" and "Hirer" | : | shall include the persons name above and their respective successors in title. | | |

## WHEREBY IT IS AGREED AS FOLLOWS:

### 1.   CHARTER PAYMENT

Agreement to let

The Owner shall let and the Hirer shall charter the Yacht for the Charter Period and the Charter Fee.

### 2.   DELIVERY OF YACHT

Delivery of Yacht

Before the Start of the Charter Period the Hirer shall have the opportunity to inspect the Yacht in company with the Owner or his agent for the purpose of ensuring that the Yacht and its equipment are in proper working order and further shall have the right to insist on a trial of at least one hour's duration. Acceptance of the yacht shall imply (prima facie) that the Yacht is in good order.

### 3.   OBLIGATIONS OF THE OWNER

Provision of documentation

The Owner hereby UNDERTAKES as follows:-

3.1 To obtain and provide any necessary documentation for the Yacht in accordance with the regulations for the time being in force under the Customs and Excise or other Acts and any amending statute, and to assist the Hirer to ensure that the Yacht is provided with the necessary ship's papers.

### 4.   OBLIGATIONS OF HIRER/S

In addition to the obligations of the Hirer in respect of insurance in Clause 5 the Hirer UNDERTAKES as follows:-

Payment of running expenses

4.1 To pay for all running expenses during the Charter Period, including the cost of charts (if not supplied), food, laundry charges, water, fuel, bills of health, harbour dues, port dues, pilotage, victuals and provisions.

146

4.2 With the exception of loss or damage arising from latent defects or from fair wear and tear, to make good all loss of or damage to any stores, gear, equipment or furnishings of every kind belonging to the Yacht caused during the Charter Period which is not recoverable under the insurance effected by the Owner as well as any loss or damage arising after the Charter Period but attributable to any act or default of the Hirer.

**Agreement not to sub-let**

4.3 Not to lend, sub-let or otherwise part with the control of the Yacht.

**Restriction of user**

4.4 Not to use the Yacht for any purpose other than private pleasure cruising for himself, his crew and his guests, nor to race the Yacht without the prior written consent of the Owner. The Hirer further undertakes not to tow any dinghy but to lash it on deck.

**Maximum number of crew**

4.5 To limit the number of the party to not more than the number of berths on the Yacht unless the Owner grants permission for a greater number.

**Cruising limits**

4.6 Not to take the Yacht outside the Cruising Limits.

**Unlawful acts**

4.7 Not knowingly or recklessly to permit to be done or to do any act which may render void the Owner's policy of insurance or result in the forfeiture of the Yacht.

**Observation of regulations**

4.8 To observe all regulations of Customs, Port, Harbour or other Authorities to which the Yacht becomes subject.

Customs
clearance

4.9  To ensure that the Yacht is properly cleared by British Customs on leaving for and returning from abroad.

5.   INSURANCE AND LIABILITIES

5.1  The Owner shall insure the Yacht for its full market value against fire and all the usual marine and collision risks with protection and indemnity cover of at least £500,000 (but not so as to cover the first [£50] of any claim or damage to sails unless caused by dismasting or collision). The Owner also undertakes to inform the appropriate broker or underwriter that the Yacht is on charter to the Hirer for the Charter Period. The Owner will provide for the Hirer/s on request a copy of the policy or certificate and shall ensure that the Hirer is covered under the policy or certificate for the same risks as the Owner himself.

5.2  The Owner shall not, however, be liable for any personal injury, or any loss of, or damage to, the personal property of the Hirer or any member of the party, or any other person invited aboard the Yacht by the Hirer during the Charter Period.

SIGNED BY THE OWNER:

SIGNED BY THE HIRER/S:

## NOTES

The French Customs Authorities will treat as a commercial vessel any craft having aboard paying guests, crew or passengers unless the craft falls into one of a limited number of exceptional categories.

One such category is a bare-boat charter where all those aboard who have contributed to the cost of the charter and voyage are parties to the charter agreement.

The purpose of this document is to evidence the charter agreement and it shall be construed in the context of any collateral or pre-existing agreement between the parties hereto.

# APPENDIX 4

# LICENSING ACT 1964

## A. SCHEDULE 5

### Requirements to be complied with by club's application for Registration Certificate

1. The application shall specify the name, objects and address of the club and shall state that there is kept at the address a list of the names and addresses of the members.

2. The application shall state, in terms of subsections (1) and (2) of section 41 of this Act, that the club is qualified under those subsections to receive a registration certificate for the premises, or will be so qualified if, as regards any provision of the rules specified in the application, the court sees fit to give a direction under section 42(2) of this Act.

3. The application shall set out, or shall incorporate a document annexed which sets out, the names and addresses of the members of any committee having the general management of the affairs of the club and those of the members of any other committee concerned with the purchase for the club or with the supply by the club of intoxicating liquor, and those of other officers of the club.

4. (1) The application shall give, or shall incorporate a document annexed which states, the rules of the club or, in the case of an application for renewal, the changes in the rules made since the last application for the issue or renewal of the certificate.
   (2) If, in the case of an application for renewal, there has been no such change as aforesaid, the application shall so state.

5. The application shall:
   (a) Identify the premises for which the issue or renewal of the registation certificate is sought; and
   (b) State the interest held by or in trust for the club in those premises and, if it is a leasehold or if the club has no interest, the name and address of any person to whom payment is or is to be made of rent under the lease or otherwise for the use of the premises.

6. (1) The application shall give, or shall incorporate a document annexed which gives:
   (a) Particulars of any property not comprised in paragraph 5 of this Schedule which is or is to be used for the purposes of the club and not held by or in trust for the club absolutely, including the name and address of any person to whom payment is or is to be made for the use of that property;
   (b) Particulars of any liability of the club in respect of the principal or interest of moneys borrowed by the club or charged on property held by or in trust for the club, including the name and address of the person to whom payment is or is to be made on account of that principal or interest;
   (c) Particulars of any liability of the club or of a trustee for the club in respect of which any person has given a guarantee or provided any security, together with particulars of the guarantee or security given or provided, including the name and address of the person giving or providing it.
   (2) An application for renewal, or document annexed to it, may give the particulars required by this paragraph by reference to the changes (if any) since the last application by the club for the issue or renewal of the registration certificate.
   (3) If there is no property or liability of which particulars are required by any paragraph or sub- paragraph (1) of this paragraph, the application shall so state.
   (4) In this paragraph, "liability" includes a future or contingent liability.

7. (1) The application shall give, or shall incorporate a document annexed which gives, particulars of any premises not comprised in paragraph 5 of this

Schedule, which have within the preceding twelve months been occupied and habitually used for the purposes of the club, and shall state the interest then held by or in trust for the club in those premises and, if it was a leasehold interest or if the club had no interest, the name and address of any person to whom payment was made of rent under the lease or otherwise for the use of the premises.

(2) If there are no premises of which particulars are required by this paragraph, the application shall so state.

8. Where the interest held by or in trust for the club in any land of which particulars are required by paragragh 5, 6 or 7 of this Schedule is or was a leasehold interest, and the rent under the lease is not or was not paid by the club or the trustees for the club, the application shall state the name and address of the person by whom it is or was paid.

## B.  SCHEDULE 6

### Procedure on applications and complaints relating to Registration Certificates

### Issue, renewal and surrender of Registration Certificates

*Applications etc.*
1. (1) An application by a club for the issue, renewal or variation of a registration certificate shall be made by lodging the application, together with the number of additional copies required under paragraph 4 of this Schedule, with the Clerk to the Justices.

(2) The court may, on such conditions as the court thinks fit, allow such an application to be amended.

(3) An amended application shall be made by lodging with the Clerk to the Justices the original application or the relevant parts of it altered so as to show the amendments, together with the number of additional copies required under paragraph 4 of this Schedule.

2. A registration certificate shall be surrendered by lodging with the Clerk to the Justices a notice of surrender, together with the certificate and such number of

additional copies of the notice as is required under paragraph 4 of this Schedule.

3. (1) Any such application or amended application and any such notice shall be signed by the chairman or by the secretary of the club.

   (2) In the absence of objection the court shall not require proof that an application or amended application purporting to be signed is duly signed.

4. On receipt of any such application or amended application or of any such notice the Clerk to the Justices shall forthwith send a copy to any chief officer of police concerned and to the Clerk of any Local Authority concerned, and the number of additional copies required to be lodged with the Clerk is the number necessary to provide the copies the Clerk needs for this purpose.

5. A club applying for the issue of a registration certificate for any premises, or for the renewal of a registration certificate in respect of different, additional or enlarged premises, shall give public notice of the application (identifying those premises and giving the name and address of the club) either:

   (a) By displaying the notice on or near the premises, in a place where it can conveniently be read by the public, for the seven days beginning with the date of the application; or

   (b) By advertisement on one at least of those days in a newspaper circulated in the place where the premises are situated.

## C.   SCHEDULE 7

### Provisions as to club rules

*Management of club*

1. The affairs of the club, in matters not reserved for the club in general meeting or otherwise for the decision of the general body of members, must, under the rules, be managed by one or more elective committees; and one committee must be a general committee, charged with the general management of those affairs in matters not assigned to special committees.

*General meetings*
2. (1) There must, under the rules, be a general meeting of the club at least once in every year, and fifteen months must not elapse without a general meeting.
   (2) The general committee must be capable of summoning a general meeting at any time on reasonable notice.
   (3) Any members entitled to attend and vote at a general meeting must be capable of summoning one or requiring one to be summoned at any time on reasonable notice, if a specified number of them join to do so; and the number required must not be more than thirty nor more than one-fifth of the total number of the members so entitled.
   (4) At a general meeting the voting must be confined to members, and all members entitled to use the club premises must be entitled to vote, and must have equal voting rights.

*Membership*
3. (1) Ordinary members must, under the rules, be elected either by the club in general meeting or by an elective committee, or by an elective committee with other members of the club added to it for the purpose; and the name and address of any person proposed for election must, for not less than two days before the election, be prominently displayed in the club premises in a part frequented by the members.
   (2) The rules must not make any such provision for the admission of persons to membership otherwise than as ordinary members as is likely to result in the number of members so admitted being significant in proportion to the total membership.

*Meaning of "elective committee"*
4. (1) In this Schedule "elective committee" means, subject to the following provisions of this paragraph, a committee consisting of members of the club who are elected in accordance with sub-paragraph (2) of this paragraph for a period of not less than one year nor more than 5 years; and paragraph 2 (4) of this Schedule shall apply to voting at the election as it applies to voting at general meetings.

(2) Elections to the committee must be held annually, and if all the elected members do not go out of office in every year, there must be fixed rules for determining those that are to; and all members of the club entitled to vote at the election and of not less than two years' standing, must be equally capable (subject only to any provision made for nomination by members of the club and to any provision prohibiting or restricting re-election) and, if nomination is required must have equal rights to nominate persons for election.

## D.   **APPLICATION FOR A REGISTRATION CERTIFICATE**

To the Magistrate's Court for the                          of

THE                               CLUB

1.  I, AB, of                          , the [chairman] [secretary] of the above-named club, make application for the [issue] [renewal] [variation] of a registration certificate.

2.  The objects of the club are [ ].

3.  The address of the club is [ ].

4.  A list of the names and addresses of the members is kept at the address given in paragraph 3 above.

5.  Under the rules of the club persons may not be admitted to membership, or be admitted as candidates for membership or to any of the privileges of membership, without an interval of at least two days between their nomination or application for membership and their admission, nor may persons becoming members without prior nomination or application be admitted to the privileges of membership without an interval of at least two days between their becoming members and their admission.

6.  The club is established and conducted in good faith and has not less than 25 members.

7. Intoxicating liquor is not supplied, or intended to be supplied, to members on the premises otherwise than by, or on behalf of, the club.

8. The purchase for the club and the supply by the club of intoxicating liquor (so far as not managed by the club in general meeting or otherwise by the general body of members) is managed by an elective committee.

9. No arrangements are, or are intended, to be made:
   (a) For any person to receive at the expense of the club any commission, percentage or similar payment on or with reference to purchases of intoxicating liquor by the club; or
   (b) For any person directly or indirectly to derive any pecuniary benefit from the supply of intoxicating liquor by or on behalf of the club to members or guests, apart from any benefit accruing to the club as a whole [and apart also from the benefit derived by members indirectly by reason of the supply giving rise to or contributing to a general gain from the carrying on of the club].

10. The club is accordingly qualified to receive a registration certificate [or will be so qualified if, as regards the provisions of rule[s] [ ] of the rules of the club, the court sees fit to give a direction under sub-section (2) of section 42 of the Licensing Act 1964].

11. The names and addresses of the members of the committee having the general management of the affairs of the club [including the purchase for the club and the supply by the club of intoxicating liquor] are [as follows:-] [set out in the document annexed hereto marked "A"].
    [The names and addresses of the members of the committee concerned with the purchase for the club or with the supply by the club of intoxicating liquor are [as follows:-] [set out in the document annexed hereto, marked "B"].]
    The names and addresses of any officers of the club not included in the above-mentioned list or lists of members are as follows:

12. The [changes in the] rules of the club [since the last application for the issue or renewal of a certificate] are [as follows:-] [set out in the document annexed hereto marked " "] [There has been no change in the rules of the club since the last application for the issue or renewal of a certificate].

13. The premises for which the [issue] [renewal] [variation] of [a] [the] registration certificate is sought consist of [ ] [and are [different from] [additional to] the premises to which the said certificate relates] [have been enlarged since the said certificate was [issued] [last renewed].]

14. The said premises are [to be] occupied by and habitually used for the purposes of the club.

15. The said premises are [to be] open to members during the following times:- The hours fixed by or under the rules of the club as the permitted hours are as follows:-

16. The interest held by or in trust for the club in the premises is [ ] [and the name and address of the person to whom payment is [to be] made of [rent under the lease] [*or as the case may be*] are as follows:-]

[17. Particulars of any property other than the premises referred to in paragraph 13 above which is [to be] used for the purposes of the club and not held by or in trust for the club absolutely, and the name and address of the person to whom payment is [to be] made for the use of that property are [as follows:-] [set out in the document annexed hereto marked " "].]
[There is no property other than the premises referred to in paragraph 13 above which is or is to be used for the purposes of the club and not held by or in trust for the club absolutely.]

18. [Particulars of any] [There is no] liability of the club in respect of the principal or interest of moneys borrowed by the club or charged on property held by or in trust for the club [and the name and address of the person to whom payment is [to be] made on account of that principal or interest are [as follows] [set out in the document annexed

157

hereto marked " "]].

19. [Particulars of any] [There is no] liability of the club or of a trustee for the club in respect of which any person has given any guarantee or provided any security [and particulars of such guarantee or security and the name and address of the person giving or providing it are [as follows] [set out in the document annexed hereto marked " "]].

*In the case of an application for renewal the paragraphs numbered 16 to 19 above may be deleted and the following paragraph substituted:*
[16. There have been no changes since the last application by the club for the issue or renewal of a registration certificate in the particulars required by paragraph 6 of Schedule 5 to the Licensing Act 1964] [except as [follows] [set out in the document annexed hereto marked " "].]
*[If the above alternative paragraph 16 is used, renumber the following paragraphs accordingly.]*

20. [Particulars of any] [There are no] premises other than those referred to in paragraph 13 above which have within the past twelve months been occupied and habitually used for the purposes of the club [and the interest held by or in trust for the club in those premises [and the name and address of the person to whom payment was made of [rent under the lease] *[or as the case may be]* are [as follows] [set out in the document annexed hereto marked " "]].

[21. *In case any such rent was not paid by the club or the trustees for the club;* The name and address of the person by whom the rent referred to in paragraphs [16, 17 or 20 *or as the case may be]* above was paid are as follows:...]

[22. The Club is a registered society within the meaning of the Industrial and Provident Societies Act 1965, or the Friendly Societies Act 1974.]
Dated the            day of                      .

*[signature of chairman or secretary]*

NOTE

Three copies of the application must be lodged with the clerk to the justices.

If the local authority are not also the fire authority, a fourth copy should also be included.

# APPENDIX 5

# TRUST DEED FOR THE TRUSTEE OWNERSHIP OF CLUB YACHTS

THIS DEED is made the [            ] day of [                    ]
19
BETWEEN
of

("the Club") and
of

("the Trustees" which expression shall include their successors in title as Trustees). The Club and the Trustees shall hereinafter be collectively referred to as "the Parties".

WHEREAS
THE CLUB proposes to place in the legal ownership of the Trustees certain craft (as hereinafter defined) and the Parties have determined to enter into this Deed to record the trusts and other provisions subject to which the Trustees shall hold the craft.

NOW THIS DEED WITNESSES as follows:
1.  IN THIS DEED the expression "the Craft" includes any one or more sailing or motor craft which shall from time to time be placed in the legal ownership of the Trustees and which the Trustees shall have acknowledged in writing that they hold upon the terms of this Deed and where the context admits the expression also includes the proceeds of sale of the Craft and any insurance moneys received in respect thereof.

2.  THE TRUSTEES HEREBY JOINTLY AND SEVERALLY COVENANT WITH THE CLUB that they shall deal with the Craft in any manner (and in particular but without prejudice to the generality of the

160

foregoing by letting or sale or other disposal) as the Club shall direct.

3.  FOR THE PURPOSE of Clause 2 a direction in writing addressed to the Trustees signed by the Secretary of the Club shall be deemed to be properly given by the Club and the Trustees shall be under no obligation to enquire as to the correctness or otherwise of any such direction.

4.  THE CLUB shall indemnify the Trustees against:
    (a) Any expenses incurred by the Trustees in carrying out any directions relating to the Craft given as aforesaid.
    (b) All expenses relating to the Craft howsover arising and in particular (but without prejudice to the generality of the foregoing) all expenses incurred in maintaining, repairing, renewing, servicing, insuring and mooring or berthing the Craft and all harbour dues and other expenses imposed upon the owners or users of the Craft by any competent authority. (c) All liabilities whatsover and howsover arising out of the ownership or use of the Craft including claims by any third party or by any user or crew of or passenger on the Craft.

AS WITNESS the Parties have hereunto set their hands and seals the day and year first before written.

SIGNED SEALED AND DELIVERED

by the Club

in the presence of:-

by the Trustees

in the presence of:-

# APPENDIX 6

# MEDIA GUIDE

Every club or class association will benefit from the appointment of a press officer or person responsible solely for the publicity for the organisation.

If boating is to be promoted and publicised, a comprehensive and regular press campaign is essential.

This media guide is designed to be an aide-memoire for those involved with the promotion of the sport at club or class level.

If you require further information or help for a specific project, please do not hesitate to contact Vicki Davies at the RYA. Useful information can also be obtained from the Yachting Journalists' Association. Write to the Secretary, Steve Anscell, 5 Ravenswood, Lower Church Road, Titchfield Common, Fareham, Hampshire PO14 4PX.

## THE MEDIA
Each press officer should look at local, national and specialist media sources to establish which is the most suitable outlet for public relations activities.

### Newspapers
National: These will concern you only if involved in an event of national or international importance. Most national dailies publish editions in Manchester and Scotland as well as in London.

Local: These can be weekly, daily, paid for or free. Whichever, one of the first things to discover is when each newspaper has its deadline — i.e. the time and day of the week after which no more news or articles will be accepted. Establish contact with the person responsible.

### Local Radio
Both independent and BBC stations will be pleased to receive news of local interest. As transmission is frequent, there are no delays and deadlines will occur several times a day. There

162

are several types of radio programme at which to aim your releases:
- — Sports programmes
- — Young people's news broadcasts
- — Chat shows
- — Phone-ins

## Regional television
This is undoubtedly the most difficult area of the media to attract. Usually only the major sports items are covered, but since 1982 when the new franchises were granted, regional news programmes have begun to take localised news more seriously.

## Specialist Press
There are a growing number of publications serving different areas of the sport, some have very large circulations, while there are many other, more localised magazines coming on to the market. Choosing the right publication is important. A list is available on request from the RYA, Woking.

## National television
National television does not give sailing as much coverage as it might. But always bear in mind, children's news and chat shows may well be interested in covering a youth event.

## HOW TO GET YOUR NEWS PUBLISHED OR HEARD
1. Check deadline dates. In the case of a monthly magazine, these can be surprisingly early. So get your material in as early as possible.
2. Get to know the editor and his reporters. A good working relationship can result in extra column inches.
3. Whenever possible, issue invitations (at least two) to each medium for all major functions and make sure journalists are looked after when they arrive.
4. Try not to talk 'off record'. If you do not want something published, why talk about it?
5. Most local papers do not have a wealth of photographers. Those they have cannot be everywhere, so supplying a good black and white photograph (good quality colour is better than nothing at all) can enhance the chance of publication. Remember to put captions on all photographs. Do not expect them to be returned.

## THE PRESS RELEASE

Timing is critical in spreading news. Key dates should be firmly logged so that, for instance, you do not miss special issues covering boat shows you are attending. Ensure dates of key events are logged with the press and are included in local event diaries.

Hold on to a piece of good news if it is fairly ageless; there may be a better time to release it. Some items, for example, the announcement of the club's thousandth new member can be delayed and combined with something such as tickets being on sale for the annual dinner.

If you strike lucky and a release gets extensive coverage which, in turn, generates a lot of enquiries, make sure the organisation is geared to handle them or you will have wasted your efforts and may alienate the press.

Aim for quality rather than quantity; over-hyping can be counter-productive.

Avoid attacking something in order to promote your own interests. If you claim that yours is the best club in the area, for example, you may only provoke others to greater efforts and, in any case, such a claim may sound boastful and off-putting.

### Presentation

Untidy or illegible releases are unlikely to be published. Type the information on one side of the paper only and always use double spacing with wide margins.

Use A4 size paper with the club or class name at the top. You could consider special 'press release' paper, possibly in a colour, to stand out on the editor's desk.

### Content

Be brief. Always begin with the most pertinent facts of the release — so that if the piece is shortened for length, as can often happen, the first few paragraphs will stand on their own. A journalist will often cut the last paragraph (or two).

An easy guideline is to answer the questions WHO, WHAT, WHEN, WHERE, WHY and HOW without the need for further reference at the beginning.

Try to avoid unexplained initials as these may confuse the harassed sub-editor, resulting in the release not being published. Give full names and ages where possible.

If there is a human interest element — a particular

celebration for the sailor, a special achievement — maximise on it. Expand the story in the main body of the text, but always keep it short and concise.

Do not blur your messages. If you are trying to make a point, do not try to get in a piece on something else too.

If you have a long and detailed story, prepare a summary release of a maximum of two pages, then include attachments going into more detail. Specialist magazines may use the detail, general press will probably only use the outline.

If a release runs to more than a page, staple them together. Do not rely on paper clips.

If you prepare biographies of competitors, and you should, include dates of birth rather than ages.

## Topping and tailing

Capture attention with a snappy headline, something which encapsulates the story.

Embargoes are a contentious area. Try not to issue a statement before you are prepared to see it in print. Although most editors will acknowledge an embargo, some may not. Always indicate clearly, at the top, the date of the release.

At the end, name the person to be contacted for further information, complete with home and work telephone numbers.

## And finally

Do not expect the release to be printed as you sent it. Always make sure you supply clear concise facts for the paper or radio to use without having to chase up more information. Do not churn out press releases for the sake of doing so. There must always be something to say which is news.

If you build a reputation as a good news source, editors will want to hear from you.

## Photographs

Photographs are important and they grab attention. Take them seriously.

To stand the best chance of getting a picture in the paper, use a black and white print, if possible featuring action rather than a formal group. If there is no alternative a good quality colour print can be used but, as a reproduction is not as clear, this is not generally preferred.

Prints for publication should be at least five inches by

seven inches and glossy. Television producers prefer matt to glossy because there is less reflection for the cameras.

All photos should have a caption on the back which clearly identifies the event and gives details of people featured.

Consider photographing winning competitors from other areas individually. A picture of each winner receiving his prize and an appropriate caption and copy sent to the local press concerned, will probably get a very high strike rate and is well worth the effort.

## THE INTERVIEW

Television and radio interviews will take place in one of the following ways:
— in a studio
— by telephone
— with a portable recorder

On the spot interviews are taped with a portable recorder. The one problem is that there is little time to prepare, so ask the reporter about probable points to be covered (he or she may not tell you what questions are to be asked) and marshall your thoughts.

Studio recordings are best and will probably help the sports editor and his staff. Should you not be able to go the studio, ask to be interviewed on the telephone. This is not ideal, because the recording is inferior and the journalist may think it gives a poor image to the listener of an important subject.

Remember that the remark 'no comment' is invariably interpreted as meaning that you have something to hide — so be positive. People are interested in what you have to say, so avoid clipped 'yes' and 'no' answers. Do not ramble and try not to be funny. If there is a silence you do not have to be the first to fill it; you may jump in nervously and say the wrong thing. If an interviewer makes an incorrect statement in his introduction or when asking a question correct it at the start of your reply. Do it courteously, but do not be side-tracked.

One word of warning. The recording will not necessarily be broadcast verbatim. It will be edited. Try to put your points over concisely so that editing will not effect what you say. Record the interview when it is broadcasted so that you can study it afterwards and learn from your mistakes.

Interviews for magazines and papers are often conducted in the same way, although they may be taken down in shorthand and are almost invariably conducted on your own ground. After an interview a journalist might show you his piece before publication so that you can check the facts. In the rare event that he does so, you should never hope or attempt to censor copy.

## THE PRESS CONFERENCE

The two most common reasons for such events are to explain something that cannot be communicated in a statement, such as visits by a sports personality or to provide the press with an opportunity to ask questions and obtain answers.

Before holding a press conference, ask if it is really necessary. Do not invite the press if a release would do perfectly well. Remember, press conferences are a waste of time and money unless they assist the press to get a better story.

Tailor the time to suit the journalists. Many find mid-week the most convenient.

The room should be large enough for the numbers expected. Invitations should be sent out as soon as possible, several days in advance for local papers, but much earlier for monthlies and should include an embargoed copy of the statement to be made for immediate publication after the conference.

Keep a register of all those attending, with the names of the publications represented, in order to follow up afterwards. The number of speakers and length of speeches should be kept to a minimum.

Over-lavish entertaining can be positively bad public relations and is often not cost-effective. What you serve is entirely up to you and the time of day. But avoid serving alcohol before a conference otherwise your guests may get drowsy, drunk or difficult. The best balance is coffee before, drinks afterwards.

Post someone on the door to greet journalists and have a signing-in system. Name badges, where necessary, should be laid out in alphabetical order with spares for unexpected guests.

It is advisable to follow up all invitations and press releases with a personal phone call.

## PRESS FACILITIES

If you have invited the press to attend an event, it is vital to make sure that certain facilities are provided exclusively for the journalists.

The most important of all is the telephone. Nothing is more irritating to a reporter than having to stand in a queue of jubilant or dejected competitors phoning home! Telephones are an important lifeline in today's journalism. So, make sure there are enough phones available for the press and that club staff, competitors and the public are not allowed to use these phones when the press may need them. The phones must be able to receive incoming phone calls, and, if they work on the new card system, these must be available to the press. Remember, when installing lines specifically for the press that the 'bleeping telephones' make modern transmission of copy impossible for those publications with electronic equipment.

A separate working area with chairs and tables, ideally located close to the competitors and the race officer, is another important facility. The provision of power points, typewriters as well as paper are necessary. Telex facilities are useful at major events, but if the club does not have a proficient operator it may be worth considering an account or pay as you use system.

Dry, fast motor boats are another facility which should be made available. The driver should not only be 'au fait' with handling the boat but should also be sympathetic to the differing needs of press and competitor alike. He must be able to keep out of the sailors' way but also provide the photographer with the best possible view.

Where there is a restricted zone, in powerboat racing for example, or there are a large number of press attending a privilege flag system for press boats situated in an optimum position is the solution.

## MONITORING MEDIA COVERAGE

Following an event always check the papers, television and radio stations you contacted, to check whether the event was covered.

Always encourage members to forward all press cuttings and note down times of television and radio coverage if these cannot be recorded and build up a press cuttings file.

A comprehensive press cuttings file will indicate just how successful you have been as well as providing an essential source for reference and a means of helping you to know how to develop your activities in the future.

## USEFUL ADDRESSES
Yachting Journalists' Association
The Secretary, Steve Anscell, 5 Ravenswood, Lower Church
Road, Titchfield Common, Fareham, Hampshire. PO14 4PX
Telephone: 04895 2201

The National Union of Journalists
Acorn House, Gray's Inn Road, London WC1
Telephone: 01-278-7916

The Institute of Journalists
Bedford Chambers, Covent Garden, London WC2E 8HA
Telephone: 01-836-6541

The Central Council of Physical Recreation
Francis House, Francis Street, London SW1P 1DE
Telephone: 01-828-3163

## MEDIA LISTS
The following media lists are available from the RYA Head
Office in any combination depending on the organisation's
needs. They can be photocopied directly on to self-adhesive
copier labels for easy use.

### National
— National media correspondents
— Powerboats journalists
— Dinghy correspondents
— Cruising correspondents
— Photographers

### Regional
— Channel Islands
— Eastern (Bedfordshire, Cambridgeshire, Essex,
Hertfordshire, Norfolk, Suffolk, E postals districts of
London)
— East Midlands (Derbyshire, Leicestershire,
Lincolnshire, Northamptonshire)
— Northern (Cleveland, Cumbria, Durham,
Northumberland, Tyne & Wear)
— North West (Cheshire, Greater Manchester,
Lancashire, Merseyside)

169

— Scotland
— South East (Kent, East Sussex, W Sussex — except Chichester Harbour, SE postal districts of London)
— South West
— Southern (Chichester Harbour, Hampshire, Isle of Wight)
— Thames Valley (Berkshire, Buckinghamshire, Oxfordshire, Surrey, London postal districts)
— Wales
— West Midlands (Hereford & Worcester, Shropshire, Staffordshire and Warwickshire)
— Yorkshire & Humberside (Humberside, North Yorkshire, South Yorkshire, West Yorkshire)
— Northern Ireland

# APPENDIX 7

# HEALTH AND SAFETY AT WORK
# ACT 1974

It is the responsibility of the [    ] YACHT CLUB to ensure, as far as is reasonably possible, the health, safety and welfare of its employees whilst at work.

The CLUB is obliged:
1.  To ensure that all fittings, fixtures and equipment are maintained in good repair and safe working order.
2.  To provide and maintain a working environment for all employees that is, as far as is reasonably practicable, safe, without risks to health, and adequate as regards facilities and arrangements for their welfare at work.

All employees have a duty under the Act:
1.  To take reasonable care of their own safety and health and that of other persons who may be affected by their acts or omissions at work.
2.  To comply with all safety procedures laid down by the [ ] Yacht Club.
3.  To report any hazard or potential hazard known to them to the Safety Officer.

**Administrative arrangements**
   The Club Secretary is the Safety Officer.

**Emergency arrangements and procedures**
1.  Fire. Notices are displayed near each fire alarm bell push and fire extinguisher. All employees should read the Fire Notice and familiarise themselves with the action to take in the event of a fire.
2.  Accidents. A First Aid box is kept in the [ ] and [ ] is in charge of the box. All accidents, including accidents to visitors, should be reported to the Safety Officer and entered in the Accident Book. All accidents will be investigated to attempt to prevent a recurrence.

# APPENDIX 8

# FORM OF LOAN NOTE ISSUED BY INCORPORATED CLUB

THE XYZ YACHT CLUB LIMITED (A COMPANY
LIMITED BY GUARANTEE) (INCORPORATED IN
ENGLAND UNDER THE COMPANIES ACT) ISSUE OF
INTEREST FREE UNSECURED LOAN NOTES
(A.D. 2017) PURSUANT TO THE MEMORANDUM
AND ARTICLES OF ASSOCIATION OF THE XYZ
YACHT CLUB LIMITED AND TO A RESOLUTION
OF THE DIRECTORS
PASSED ON THE [    ] DAY OF [         ] 1987

1.  THE XYZ YACHT CLUB LIMITED ("the Company")
    will on the 31st day of December 2017 or on such earlier
    dates as the principal moneys hereby covenanted to be
    paid ("the Principal Sum") shall become liable to be
    repaid in accordance with the conditions endorsed
    hereon, pay [        ] to [        ] of [        ] or
    other the registered holder or holders for the time being
    hereof ("the Noteholder") the sum of £[      ] (the
    Principal Sum).

2.  THIS NOTE is issued subject to and with the benefit of
    the conditions endorsed hereon which are to be deemed to
    form part of this Note.
    Given under the Common Seal of the Company this
    [     day of     ] 1987.
    THE COMMON SEAL OF THE XYZ YACHT CLUB
    LIMITED was hereunto affixed in the presence of:
    DIRECTOR
    SECRETARY

## NOTES

1.  This note is one of a series of interest free Unsecured
    Loan Notes 2017 for up to a maximum principal amount
    of £25,000. The Company shall not issue any other Note
    which would form part of a series with these Notes

172

without the prior consent in writing of all the Noteholders. All Notes shall rank pari passu inter se without preference or priority over each other.

2. Upon these Notes being repaid or purchased by the Company this Note shall be cancelled and the Company shall not be at liberty to keep the same alive for the purpose of re-issue nor to re-issue the same.

3. (a) This note shall be freely transferable by purchase and sale or otherwise to any person for the time being a full member of the XYZ Club Limited but any transfer of this Note shall be delivered to and shall be issued to the person entitled pursuant to such transfer.
   (b) Notice in writing of transfer shall be given to the Company within 28 days from any such transfer taking place by lodging with the Company the transfer together with such reasonable evidence of title as the Company may reasonably require.

4. On the death of a sole or sole surviving Noteholder prior to the said thirty-first day of December 2017 his/her personal representative shall be repaid the Principal Sum at the expiration of three calendar months after previous notice in writing requiring the Company to do so.

5. The Company reserves the right at any time prior to the said thirty-first day of December 2017 to repay in whole or in part all or any of the Notes forming part of this series such Note or Notes to be determined by lot drawn by the Company in such manner as it may from time to time decide but the Noteholders for the time being shall be entitled to attend the drawing of the lot.

6. The Principal Sum shall immediately become repayable in each and every of the following events namely:
   (a) If the Company shall go into liquidation (whether voluntary or compulsory).
   (b) If the Company is unable to pay its debts within the meaning of Section 223 of the Companies Act 1948 or shall stop payment or shall cease or threaten to cease to carry on its business.

(c) If an encumbrancer shall take possession, or a receiver or any other similar officer shall be appointed, of the assets of the Company or any part thereof.

(d) Upon the expiration of not less than three months previous notice given by the Company to the Noteholder (such repayment to be made by the Company without a premium).

7. The Company shall keep a Register of the Notes forming the series showing:
(a) The name and address of the Noteholder;
(b) The nominal amount of the Note;
(c) The serial number of the Note and the date of issue thereof;
(d) Details of each transfer of the Note; and
(e) Details of any repayment.
Any change of address of the Noteholder shall forthwith be notified to the Company. The Noteholder shall be at liberty at all reasonable times to inspect the Register and to take copies or extracts thereof at his own expense.

8. The payment by the Company of any unclaimed monies into a separate account in the name of the Company shall not constitute the Company a trustee in respect thereof and any such monies unclaimed after a period of 12 years from the due date of payment shall be forfeited and shall revert to the Company notwithstanding that in the intervening period the obligation to pay the same may have been provided for in the books of account or other records of the Company.

9. All or any of the rights for the time being attached to the Note may from time to time (whether or not the Company is being wound up) be altered with the consent of the Company given by resolution of the Directors and with the sanction of the Noteholder.

10. Any notice required to be given under this Note shall in the case of a notice to the Company be deemed to be duly served if left at or sent by post to the registered office for the time being of the Company and, in the case of notice to the Noteholder, if left at or sent by post to the address

of the Noteholder or, in the case of joint Noteholders, the address of the first named on the Register. Any such notice shall be deemed to be served at the time when the same is left at the address of the party to be served or if sent by first post at the expiration of 48 hours after the same was posted by first class prepaid Recorded Delivery post.

# APPENDIX 9

# PUBLIC ENQUIRIES

## A  GENERAL

Planning appeals, Harbour Revision Orders, Coast Protection Act Applications, Works Licences, Harbour Act Proposals and Opposed Byelaw Applications may all result in the holding of a Public Enquiry at which it may be necessary or desirable for a club to be represented.

Where a question of wide public concern or important precedent is involved, the legal committee of the RYA will often delegate RYA staff to attend and appear on behalf of, or in conjunction with, an interested club or area association.

In other circumstances it will be up to the club or association to make the running itself and it is hoped the following notes will be of assistance.

The purpose of appointing an Inspector to hear evidence at a public enquiry and report back is to give the Minister or Department concerned both a fuller picture of the issues involved than could be gained simply by correspondence and written reports, and also the benefit of the personal judgement and advice of the Inspector on the issues.

To obtain the greatest benefit from attendance at an enquiry, club representatives should keep in mind the following points:

## 1.  What is the policy of the club on the issue?

If possible a minuted decision of the management committee (or a general meeting of all members in the event of a major issue) should be taken. If a person is appointed to represent the club, he should limit himself to dealing with issues affecting the club.

## 2.  Who within the Club/Association is responsible for the conduct of the enquiry?

Duplication of effort and evidence is not only a waste of time but annoying to an inspector who ideally looks to a single source of information on each point of view. By all means have a number of different witnesses (about which more later) but only to give evidence on different aspects of the problem. Here again, duplication between witnesses is counter-productive.

### 3.  What other persons/bodies are to be represented and how will their case support or undermine yours?

If possible all those with a similar case should appoint a single representative who should have responsibility for selecting witnesses, collating evidence, editing witness statements and preparing and presenting the case. If such co-operation is not possible or desirable, at least ensure a free exchange of information at an early stage in preparation so that the case of neither party is undermined by the other.

### 4.  Who are the witnesses to be?

#### 4.1  *Local witnesses as to fact and opinion*

Detailed comments on case presentation are given below, but an early and crucial decision concerns choice of witnesses. Inspectors are professionals, but are also human, and are more likely to be impressed by a witness who can tell his story with a bit of personal style, rather than one who is as dry as dust. The ideal witness will be a local person who can show he is in touch with local opinion (eg. flag officer or past flag officer of a local club with family and business ties in the area) and is articulate, credible, capable of being objective, not too dogmatic but firm enough and knowledgable enough to stand up to a close, thorough and possibly acid cross-examination which may take him away from the topics dealt with in his own evidence.

If one person can be found who can speak authoritatively on all matters of local concern, then that is to be preferred to having a number of duplicating or conflicting witnesses.

#### 4.2  *Expert witnesses*

In any enquiry involving the construction of works, or change of use of a harbour or estuary, or introduction of byelaws, the Inspector will need to hear expert evidence as to what is the likely physical effect of the works (eg. changes in current or situation) or comparisons with other areas in the country. The promoters will have dug deep into their pockets to produce an authority on the subject, probably with a multitude of letters after his name, and the only way to match the weight given to such evidence will be to have an independent expert of your own.

Independence is essential in this context and it is therefore a mistake to enrol a local person as this will inevitably create a suspicion of bias in the inspector's mind.

Expertise can normally be discovered by a bit of imaginative research. There are literally thousands of semi-retired professionals from all walks of life who are only too pleased to take on public enquiry work, have good experience of enquiry procedures and whose fees will be hundreds rather than the thousands charged by the promoters' practising experts. It may take weeks or months to find, and brief, the right person, so an early start is essential if you are to get the most benefit from his expertise.

## 5.    Assembling the "Team"

### 5.1    *The leader*

Once the area association, action group or club committee has passed the necessary resolution and lodged the objection, and it is clear that a public enquiry will be ordered, one member of the committee should be selected to conduct the case. He should preferably have good secretarial facilities (word processors and photocopiers are now an essential part of the democratic process) and a free hand to make day-to-day decisions on the preparation of the case, if necessary reporting fortnightly or so to a sub-committee or working party. He will ideally be someone with experience of court or public enquiry procedure and with the time available to do a thorough job. This will involve the presentation of the case, cross-examination of the other side's witnesses, and introduction and "management" of your own witnesses, together with the final summing-up of your side's case. It will possibly involve a number of days' attendance at the enquiry and thus a self-employed or retired person is indicated.

### 5.2    *The secretary*

The amount of paper generated at an enquiry can be phenomenal; at airport planning enquiries it is not unusual to see crates of papers arriving in furniture vans. The advent of word processors and photocopiers has exaggerated the production of paper but has removed much of the drudgery involved.

The duties of the secretary will include typing up the draft witness statements, subsequent amendments (dating each draft), acting as post box for all correspondence, receiving and copying the other side's statements of case and witness statements, and colating all papers received before, during and after the enquiry. These can best be handled by the creation of a number of separate files, dealt with at para. 6 below.

### 5.3   Local witnesses

This person or persons will be key team members and they should start preparing their witness statements as soon as possible after the decision to hold an enquiry has been taken. It will be very evident at the enquiry which witnesses have considered their evidence carefully in advance, and which have done a rushed job in the last 48 hours before the enquiry. Advice on the preparation of statements is given at para. 9 below.

### 5.4   Expert witness

A well chosen expert witness will be able to fulfill a number of roles. In the first case he will be able to advise the leader on the validity of the objector's case, highlighting the strengths and weaknesses, and even advising that the objection should be extended, modified or dropped altogether. He will also be able to give an authoritative opinion at the enquiry, and advise the leader on the cross-examination of the other side's expert(s). He should be available at least on all the "technical" days of the enquiry. He will be the paid member of the team and it is essential to organise his fees and arrange the budget with the controlling committee at an early stage.

### 5.5   Other witnesses

There is always room at enquiries for one or two brief "cameo" parts. At a recent harbour enquiry one of the star turns was a young mother whose children had recently started Optimist sailing and whose very lives could have been put at risk by the threatened development. Emotive stuff that was the more effective coming from someone not part of the main team but appearing as a separate party rather than as an extra witness for the leading party. It is useful to know in advance who they are, what they are likely to say, and not to steal their thunder.

## 6.  Paperwork

Thorough preparation of the paperwork is the key to a professional and well organised show. This is where a well-organised secretary comes into his/her own. Access to the right equipment is also essential.

A number of files should be opened. Each of these will expand beyond recognition and relevant papers should not be muddled.

6.1   Master file, to include all documents of record, for example:

(i)   Copy minuted decision to lodge objection;
(ii)  Copy formal letter of objection;
(iii) Copy constitution of action group or letters of authority from constituent clubs of the action group;
(iv)  Correspondence with Ministry regarding arrangements for the enquiry.

6.2   Promoters' file to include:

(i)   Copy of application for scheme which is being opposed;
(ii)  Copy of "statement of case", supporting reports and witness statements. (This file will be built up in the course of the enquiry; lever arch files and a hole puncher will be essential equipment.)

6.3   Own party's file to include:

(a)   Copy formal letter of objection;
(b)   Copy of "statement of case" that may be requested by the Ministry some weeks before the hearing to help them define the issues. (This must of course be prepared after having seen the promoter's statement of case, and serves as a formal written reply);
(c)   Copy of current draft of each own witness statement;
(d)   Copy of statement of case of supporters and of supporters' witness statements.

6.4   Correspondence with own side, witnesses etc.
6.5   Correspondence with other side.
6.6   Press reports file.

## 7.  Formal letter of objection

(Specimen attached at Appendix 9B)

This must be lodged within the time allowed for objections, give details of the body making the objection and its standing, identify the proposal objected to and the general nature of the objection and reserve the right to give more details of the objection at a later stage.

It is important that the objection is made upon grounds that lie within the objector's terms of reference. For instance, "damage to wildlife habitat" is clearly nothing to do with a yacht club. If members feel strongly about that aspect they should support the local conservation group.

All points of objection should be referred to, at least briefly. A witness who is asked in cross-examination why a point he has made was not referred to in the letter of objection or statement of case is unlikely to impress the Inspector.

A formal letter of objection will typically run to no more than one side of A4.

## 8.  Statement of case

Although the Ministry will not call for a statement of case more than a couple of weeks before the enquiry and after the objectors have had a chance to take in the promoter's statement of case, it is as well to start agreeing a draft well in advance. This will enable the committee and the expert witness to consider the points at issue and to pick up any weak points in the case. It is no good objecting to a "loss of mooring area" if alternative sites are available or most of the moorings are unoccupied. Similarly, it is no good arguing that a new wall or dock will cause dangerous currents if your expert agrees with the promoters' engineers that currents will be increased by only 1/10 knot. The statement of case is therefore an important tool in defining and preparing the support for your case.

The final statement of case will normally run to no more than four sides of A4.

## 9.  Witness statements

When the hearing is over and the Inspector goes home to prepare his report (which will usually take months) his main interest will centre on the witness statements read in conjunction with his notebook. It is therefore essential that the statements in their final form are complete, well argued, accurate as to facts and reasoned as to opinion, and legible.

The statements must be typed on A4 paper, double spaced, single-sided (approx 200-250 words per page). Paragraphs should be short, with as many headings and sub-headings as possible. Each written paragraph should be numbered as the heading and sub-heading (eg. 1.1, 1.2, 2.1, 2.2, 2.3 ....)

A form of skeleton witness statement is given at Appendix 9C.

In preparing a witness statement, bear in mid that the Inspector is there to hear all the evidence and nothing is gained by skipping over important points in an effort to be brief. Brevity has its place, but not at the expense of relevant details being omitted.

Any reference to numbers, statements of fact etc. should be evidenced in the appendices to the witness statement (which should be indexed). The statement or its appendices should, if necessary, have any illustrations, charts, plans etc. in a separate brightly coloured folder no larger than A3 size. A copy of any crucial plans or charts should be available for pinning up on a board alongside the Inspector's desk, half-facing the hall for ease of reference during examination in chief and cross-examination. The illustrations folder should also be indexed and supported by a schedule at the end of the witness statement, before the other appendices.

The main witness statement will normally run to something between 15 and 50 sides of A4 depending on the complexity of the case, excluding appendices and maps etc.

## 10.  Expert witness statements

The witness will usually have a good idea of how to lay out a statement, and the emphasis to be laid on his qualifications, experience and relevant history. He should ideally have had a good look at the promoters' expert evidence and be in a position to comment on it. Also useful is the ability to point to parallel cases in the past or elsewhere in the world/country where, contrary to promises, a development has had a contrary effect, or a desired effect has been achieved in a more acceptable way.

The statement should be headed, typed and numbered in the same way but will usually be shorter as the strength of the witness will be his ability to ad-lib (giving time for the Inspector to take any necessary notes) and to respond positively to questions in cross-examination.

## 11.   Production of documents

The Inspector will expect to have read the statements of case well in advance of the hearing, and also to have received copies of the promoters' witness statements. It is not normally possible to produce your own final witness statements in advance since they will be subject to numerous amendments in response to the evidence given by the other side, and will probably only be "published" in their final form a few hours before your winesses are heard.

Thus the formal objection and statement of case will go to the Ministry, the promoters, and the local press and radio.

The final draft of the witness statements will need to be given to all those attending the enquiry; at least 10 copies and up to 25 may be required. These should be handed out by the secretary as the witness takes the stand, to the Inspector (and his assessor if present) to each barrister and solicitor, to the press, and the remainder around the public seats. It will not be necessary to duplicate the separate map folder for the press or public.

## 12.   Leader's notebook

A substantial A4 book with a front index is a useful means of keeping tabs on the paperwork. The first few pages will be a schedule of maps, plans, significant letters, press reports etc. for easy reference. The rest will be a note of proceedings and in particular of off-the-cuff comments or replies to cross-examination which do not appear in the witness statements.

## 13.   Conduct of the enquiry

The time and place of the enquiry will be notified to the secretary by the Ministry in good time. Those required to attend should immediately be notified and "booked" for the days in question. Very often the Inspector will want to have a pre-enquiry meeting solely to discuss the timetable and order of appearance. He will want to know the identity of the objectors, who is representing them, how many witnesses, and how long their case will take. So far as time estimates are concerned, each witness will give his evidence in 2 or 3 times the time taken to read his statement at a steady pace (the extra time to allow for cross-examination) and time must be allowed for the leaders' opening and closing statements. On a planning or byelaw enquiry it will be unlikely that the main objector with 3 or 4 witnesses will get through in less than 1 day (5 or 6 hours of enquiry time). If the questions are less complex, half a day may suffice.

The order of hearing should, so far as possible, be arranged so that the promoter is heard first, and the main objector heard before the others. This will give you the chance to respond to the promoter's arguments and make your mark before the enquiry is distracted by the irrelevant and time-wasting objectors who will inevitably turn up to test the Inspector's patience.

On the day in question you should arrive early and take as much table space as you will need (the more the better). Make your number with the enquiry clerk, and with the solicitor acting for the other side. You will normally be requested to sign an attendance register at the back of the hall, as will all those attending.

The first business of the enquiry will be to record those appearing and for the Inspector to note who is represented and by whom. He will then go through his proposed timetable and will adjust it where necessary to accommodate the availability of witnesses etc.

He will then call upon the promoters' Counsel to open the case. This will usually be a non-contentious scene-setting exercise and may take some hours.

Following the opening, the promoters' Counsel will call his witnesses to give evidence. This will usually also be handed round in written form and may indeed have been circulated some days earlier. In the case of factual evidence, a careful note should be made of all points which are not agreed between the parties. One of the functions of an expert witness (if you have one on your side) is to go through the evidence, marking up the points that are not agreed and noting what questions he wishes to be put to the promoters' witnesses in cross-examination.

Following his evidence-in-chief each witness will then be available for cross-examination by the objectors. The idea of this exercise is not to reduce the victim to a quivering wreck admitting to bribery and lies but rather to lay the ground for your own witnesses who will be giving evidence later. It is sufficient merely to ask the question on each point, challenge the answer, and then go on to the next point.

After cross-examination, and questions from the Inspector, the witness may be re-examined by his own Counsel on points that have arisen in the course of cross-examination. Sometimes this is taken as an opportunity to ask questions or introduce new topics that were for some reason omitted in the witness's examination-in-chief. This should not be permitted and any attempt to do so should be challenged immediately.

Once the promoters' witnesses have finished, the objectors may present their case in turn, preferably in accordance with the timetable agreed with the Inspector at the outset.

The Inspector will have seen your statement of case and will expect to hear all he needs to know from your witnesses, so your opening should be limited to a summary of your proposed witnesses and the subject-matter they are to cover. The procedure for examination of witnesses is the same for objectors as for promoters. Although the rules governing evidence in public enquiries are very much less formal than in court proceedings, it is important not to "lead" your witness on contentious statements. In other words while you may well say "Is your name John Smith? Are you the Commodore of Porttown Sailing Club, having lived and sailed in the town for 30 years?" and so on, it would be wrong to say "...and do you find the scheme objectionable on the grounds of danger to racing dinghies and cruising yachts?" Matters of opinion should be left for the witness himself to introduce.

Following the cross-examination of each witness, if you feel that he has not had a chance of giving a full reply to each question, the re-examination will give you a chance to undo some of the damage inflicted by hostile questioning. This is not an opportunity to introduce new topics but rather to sweep up loose ends from the cross-examination.

After the objectors' witnesses have been heard, the Inspector will hear closing speeches. Although there are no rules as to the order of speeches, it is conventional to take the promoters' last. This will be your chance to "wrap up" all the evidence, giving it a favourable angle where possible and highlighting the weaknesses in the promoters' evidence. Any statement or assertion made by you that has not been given in evidence will be disregarded (and probably objected to by the promoters' Counsel). As a general rule, an Inspector will start fidgeting if a closing speech goes on for more than 30 minutes, unless it is a good one dealing with complex and contradictory points of evidence.

Following closing speeches the Inspector may wish to arrange a site inspection with a representative from each party. Although in theory this will not be an opportunity for more advocacy or argument, it is important that a knowledgeable local attends to ensure that the Inspector does not receive any misleading impressions or information from others present.

After the closing of the enquiry a break of between six and twelve months can be expected before the publication of the Minister's decision and the Inspector's report.

## B.   FORMAL LETTER OF OBJECTION

Dear Sir,

### Porttown Harbour Revision Order 1987

As you will know, the Porttown Harbour Users Association represents the interests of all recreational users of the harbour areas, having in its membership the Porttown Sailing Club, the Porttown Regatta Committee, the Porttown Sea Anglers' Club and the Porttown Sub-Aqua Club as well as the local Sea Scouts' and Sea Cadets' groups.

The Harbour Users Association, and its constituent members, represent the interests of some 750 individuals who have a direct interest in the use and management of Porttown Harbour.

The proposals contained within the draft revision order referred to above are of particular concern to our members and at their meeting of [ ] 1987 the committee of the Porttown Harbour Users Association resolved to make a formal objection to the said Order.

The grounds upon which this objection is made are as follows:
(1) The proposed works will cause siltation, increased commercial traffic, interference with established tidal flows, loss of moorings, interference with and danger to navigation;
(2) The proposed powers are unnecessarily wide and irrelevant to the management of a recreational harbour;
(3) The proposed constitutional changes take insufficient account of the changed use of the harbour in recent years and in particular allow inadequate representation to recreational users.
Furthermore we reserve the right to make more detailed

observations in the context of this objection.

Yours faithfully,
Secretary, Porttown Harbour Users Association.

## C.   SKELETON WITNESS STATEMENT

### Introduction

1.1 My name is John Adams, I am a resident of Porttown and have lived here for 25 years. I am a former commodore of Porttown Sailing Club and have raced and cruised yachts and dinghies in the area every season since 1965. I hold a yachtmaster offshore ticket, run night school classes in seamanship and have been responsible for the past 10 years for the cadet training scheme within the club. I am currently treasurer of the Porttown area association of yacht clubs . . . . . . . . . . .

1.2 My evidence will demonstrate that the promoters' proposal scheme will have a substantial and adverse effect on the quality of sailing, both for cruising and racing people in the river . . . . . . . . .

### Sailing activity in the estuary
2.1 . . . . . . .

### How it is feared the scheme will affect our activities
3.1 . . . . . . .

# APPENDIX 10

# ROLE AND ORGANISATION OF THE ROYAL YACHTING ASSOCIATION

The Royal Yachting Association was founded in 1875 as the Yacht Racing Association by a number of the leading yacht clubs as a vehicle for the consolidation of the various sets of yacht racing rules and measurement rules in use around the country. In 1947 the General Purposes Committee was instituted, with a remit to monitor any government, local government, trade or other activity that may affect yachting interests, and to advise, lobby and where appropriate take direct action in defence of those interests.

The growth of the Royal Yachting Association (as it became known in 1952) over the past 30 years has reflected the growth in participation in the many branches of the sport. There are now some 1500 affiliated clubs and class associations, 1200 recognised teaching establishments and over 65000 individual personal members.

The Association is governed by a Council of 42 persons of whom 12 are elected by the personal members, 20 by the clubs voting according to their geographical region, the Chairman of the Class Association Committee and 9 ex-officio Divisional Chairmen and other co-opted members.

The detailed work of administering and protecting the sport is carried out by a number of Divisional Committees and sub-committees whose responsibilities are as follows :

## 1. DEVELOPMENT DIVISIONAL COMMITTEE

To increase the membership of the RYA and the benefits of membership by improving communications and introducing new activities and services.

To ensure that the RYA is well represented at all major yachting events (displays, shows, championships, open meetings etc.)

The production of all RYA publications including handbooks, year books and RYA News.

## 2.  GENERAL PURPOSES DIVISIONAL COMMITTEE

To represent the interests of yachtsmen, to protect their rights and encourage the orderly expansion of facilities for all forms of yachting activity.

To represent the yachting viewpoint on all proposed or existing legislation, involving liaison with Central and Local Government at all levels and negotiations with other bodies and groups of all kinds whose activities have an effect on yachtsmen.

To serve yacht clubs by supplying expertise, advice and information on matters of common interest and in particular legal matters.

## 3.  POWERBOAT RACING DIVISIONAL COMMITTEE

To promote all forms of powerboat racing and encourage an orderly development of this sport.

To co-ordinate the work of technical and specialised sub- committees.

## 4.  TRAINING DIVISIONAL COMMITTEE

To improve the standards of safety and competence in the use of all recreational craft.

To ensure that existing training schemes are efficiently managed.

To increase the scope of present training schemes and make training facilities more widely available.

To introduce and promote new or modified training schemes in order to serve additional classes of boat users.

## 5.  YACHT RACING DIVISIONAL COMMITTEE

To promote racing under sail in all its forms and encourage an orderly development of the sport.

To encourage and co-ordinate the development of the rules governing yacht racing and defining restricted and one- design classes.

To maintain records of all international and national sailing classes in this country.

To co-ordinate the work of its sub-committees, including the Racing Rules Committee, the Cruiser Racer Committee and the Race Training Committee.

## 6.  REGIONAL COMMITTEES
### Communications
(a) To establish and maintain a system of communications between the regional association and all clubs and associations within the region.
(b) To maintain constant communication with RYA Head Office.
(c) To distribute or assist in distributing RYA information to clubs and associations and to keep RYA Head Office in constant touch with events and feeling in the clubs and associations.

### Membership
(a) To keep a record of all RYA affiliated and fully affiliated clubs and associations in the region.
(b) To maintain pressure on all yacht clubs and associations in the region which are not affiliated to the RYA to become so.

### Facilities
(a) To complete records of all water and other yachting facilities in the region.
(b) To establish the existence or otherwise of deficiencies in the provision of yachting facilities in the region.
(c) To establish and maintain communications with RYA appointees to Sports Council, harbour or other official committees, bodies or authorities.

### Training
(a) To carry out or assist in carrying out in the region the training schemes developed by the Training Division.
(b) To encourage and coordinate the establishment of training schemes within the clubs and associations in the region.

### Yacht Racing
To assist the Yacht Racing Division in the establishment in the region of training schemes for:
(a) measurers;
(b) protest committees, juries, etc;
(c) race officers, regatta committees etc. and to promote the Race Training Programme.

**Powerboat Racing**
To be prepared to assist the work of the Powerboat Division when called upon.

**Legal & General Purposes**
(a) To watch the interests of all yachtsmen within the region.
(b) To keep RYA Head Office constantly informed of Local Authority and other official activity in the region which infringes or may infringe the rights and interests of yachtsmen.
(c) To assist the General Purposes Division in its work of protecting and furthering yachtsmen's interests and, where appropriate, to negotiate with Local Authorities and other official bodies on behalf of yachtsmen.

7.  **REGIONAL CHAIRMEN'S COMMITTEE**
To co-ordinate the activities of the RYA Regions and to act as a forum for the exchange of views between regions and between regions and RYA headquarters. To maintain a liaison with the Sports Council at regional level.

This independent committee is not a subcommittee of the Council but a forum of all chairmen of the RYA regional committees which are autonomous groupings of RYA affiliated clubs each with their own constitution independent of the RYA.

# APPENDIX 11

# INSPECTION OF INSURANCE CERTIFICATES BY CLUBS MANAGING RACING

Following the introduction of the Unfair Contract Terms Act 1977, clubs were warned that by inspecting competitors' insurance certificates, they may be laying themselves open to the risk of legal action in the event that an invalid certificate is overlooked and a fellow competitor or his or her yacht is injured or damaged by the uninsured competitor. This warning still remains valid. The following points should be noted:

1. The Act applies to "businesses". To the extent that a yacht club's activities constitute a business, the Act will be relevant. As a result, the usual "Notice of Disclaimer" appearing on club notice boards, exonerating the club from liability for negligence, may not necessarily be valid. That is not to say that such notices should be removed, but simply that they may not give a club the protection which might otherwise be assumed.

2. The main provisions of the Act may be summarised as follows:
   (a) An organisation can no longer, whether by a term in a contract or a public notice, exclude or restrict its liability for death or personal injury caused by its negligence.
   (b) An organisation can only exclude or restrict its liability for any other damage (i.e. property damage) caused by its negligence in so far as the exclusion or restriction of liability is in all the circumstances "reasonable".

3. Where a club regularly inspects insurance certificates, a negligent omission to ensure that a competitor has a valid certificate may lay the club open to a legal action. For example, a competitor who is injured (or whose boat is damaged) by an uninsured competitor may allege that the

club, having made it known that competitors' insurance certificates are regularly checked, thereby undertook a duty towards other competitors to ensure that all competitors' certificates would be valid and that all competitors complied with any insurance declarations. As a result of the club's negligent breach of this duty, the injured competitor has suffered loss in so far as he or she is unable to recover damages from the uninsured competitor. This loss, the injured party might say, should be recoverable from the club.

Whether or not a court would uphold such a line of argument, it is clear that a clause which seeks to exclude or restrict the club's liability for this type of incident is unlikely to be effective.

4.  If a club wishes to continue inspecting competitors' certificates, then it should check with its own insurers that it is covered for any claims which might be made against the club for death, personal injury or damage to property taking place during events in circumstances where the club may have negligently failed to check valid insurance cover.

5.  It is for these reasons that the RYA's Standard Sailing Instructions include, at clause 2.1, the following phrase: "The safety of a yacht and her entire management *including insurance* shall be the sole responsibility of the owner/competitor racing the yacht . . . . ." If a club adopts a policy of inspecting insurance certificates, some of this responsibility is likely to revert to the club.

6.  In order to encourage competitors to maintain third party insurance cover, we suggest that a written declaration is signed by all competitors along the following lines:

"I . . . . declare that I hold valid and current boat insurance which covers me for third party claims whilst racing and that I will continue to do so whilst engaged in racing at the . . . Sailing Club.

Signed . . . . . . . . . . .

Date . . . . . . . . . . . ."